The Quilter's Start-to-Finish Workbook

The Quilter's Start-to-Finish Workbook

Margit Echols

Former title: The Quilter's Coloring Book

BARNES & NOBLE BOOKS

A DIVISION OF HARPER & ROW, PUBLISHERS

New York, Cambridge, Philadelphia
San Francisco, London, Mexico City
São Paulo, Sydney

A previous edition of this book was published by Thomas Y. Crowell Company, under the title *The Quilter's Coloring Book*.

THE QUILTER'S START-TO-FINISH WORKBOOK. Copyright © 1979 by Margit Echols. All rights reserved. Printed in the United States of America. No part of this book may be used or reproduced in any manner whatsoever without written permission except in the case of brief quotations embodied in critical articles and reviews. For information address Harper & Row, Publishers, Inc., 10 East 53rd Street, New York, N.Y. 10022. Published simultaneously in Canada by Fitzhenry & Whiteside Limited, Toronto.

First BARNES & NOBLE BOOKS edition published 1983.

Library of Congress Cataloging in Publication Data

Echols, Margit.
The quilter's start-to-finish workbook.

Reprint. Originally published: The quilter's coloring book. New York : Crowell, c1979.
1. Quilting—Patterns. I. Title.
TT835.E37 1983   746.9'7   83-47967
ISBN 0-06-463589-9 (pbk.)

83 84 85 86 10 9 8 7 6 5 4 3 2 1

To my mother and father

Special thanks to Stu, whose support and
encouragement caused it to happen,

To Helen Merrill, who never gave up,

And to my editor, Carol Cohen, who really knows her stuff.

CONTENTS

11/INTRODUCTION

13/QUILTING BASICS

33/THE QUILT DESIGNS

If you copy a quilt exactly, you know how it will turn out. But if you change any of the colors, you can't be sure what will happen to the design until the quilt is almost finished. A color affects the value, the intensity, and even the apparent size of the colors next to it. Changes in color can transform a traditional quilt into a strikingly modern one, or soften a bright or busy quilt to one with muted tones.

For examples of how very different the same quilt design looks in different colors, turn to the color plates following the next section. You will see that the Log Cabin can be modern or traditional, boldly colored or gently shaded; you will also see that an arrangement of darker colors next to each other can create a diamond shape. At first glance you might not even realize that the two Pineapple quilts are stitched from the same pattern. And the quilts of the Hexagon design illustrate that a quilt can consist of repeated areas, or the entire quilt can be given a single motif.

So that you can create your own quilt, *The Quilter's Start-to-Finish Workbook* gives you four pages to color for each of twenty quilt designs. The whole design is drawn, not just one quilt block. You will be able to see the relationships of the colors you choose in a complete quilt.

How you choose your colors and how you put them together is limited only by your imagination. Because the designs in this book are printed blank, without the colors and densities you're used to, they will suggest many unconventional and exciting new possibilities. You can experiment with color, test your own ideas.

To color, use an instrument with a fairly fine point such as a colored pencil or a water-based felt-tip pen. These can be found in a wide selection of colors in most stationery and art supply stores. Oil-based felt-tipped pens tend to leak through the paper. The blank designs are printed back to back, so don't use pens that bleed through. Pastels or crayons are not as suitable, because the points get thick. Once you've colored a design to your satisfaction, use it as a guide in cutting and sewing your quilt.

The patterns included for each quilt design are drawn to size. You won't need graph paper or any drafting tools; the patterns can be used as they are. And they are followed by step-by-step illustrated sewing instructions.

Most of the designs are easy to assemble. A note at the beginning of each set of sewing instructions will alert you to any complicated sewing required. Instructions for these more difficult sewing techniques, such as turning corners or sewing curved seams, are fully described in the beginning of this book. Read the sections that follow before starting your quilt. They contain all a beginning or advanced quilter needs to know to complete the sewing of any of the designs in the book.

QUILTING BASICS

The patterns in *The Quilter's Start-to-Finish Workbook* have been drawn to size. You don't have to enlarge them and you don't have to add seam allowances. Just cut them out directly from the pages. If you don't want to cut up the book, trace the patterns and cut out the tracings. Be sure to write the number of each piece and the name of the quilt on your copies, especially if you might use the patterns over again.

If you plan to use the patterns again, mount them one page at a time with permanent spray glue or rubber cement on heavy paper or cardboard before cutting them out. Rubber cement will dry out after a time, so use the permanent spray glue if you want to store the patterns. Always cut carefully. A bad cut will plague you at each step in assembling the quilt.

This drawing is of a typical quilt pattern piece. The seam allowance lines on all pattern pieces in this book are drawn ¼ inch from the sewing line. With this size seam allowance you can stitch the final quilting top stitches close to the seam line. Some quilters prefer seam allowances of ½ inch because they're easier to sew. If you'd rather have wide seams, add ¼ inch all the way around each piece, but remember that it will be more difficult to quilt by hand through the quilt top, the seam allowances, and the other layers when you've finished.

The pattern pieces have been drawn with squared-off corners so that the ends of the pieces will match when sewn together and you won't have to trim off any excess fabric.

The straight line you see drawn through the seam allowance is a notch. Notches are

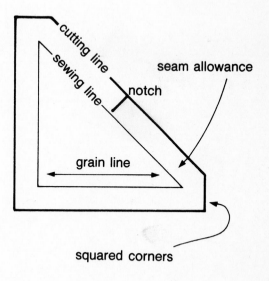

added to help you line up pieces accurately before sewing. After cutting out a pattern piece, be sure to clip all notches. Don't be afraid to clip to just short of the sewing line on curved pieces. If you don't clip deep enough, the seam will pull and the quilt block will not lie flat.

You will find arrows on triangular pattern pieces and other pieces with bias edges. Line these arrows up with the fabric's grain lines, the vertical or horizontal threads of the fabric. The vertical threads are parallel to the selvages; you may find it easier simply to place the pattern pieces with the arrows parallel to the selvages. Square or oblong pieces don't need arrows. Just line up any of the straight sides of these pieces with the grain of the fabric.

Be sure to watch the grain lines when laying out the pattern pieces. If you don't, the fabric will pull and no amount of ironing will flatten the bubbles.

FABRIC

Fabrics that work best for quilts are firmly woven, flexible, soft in texture, and, most important of all, of good quality. You'll be putting many hours of work into your quilt. Poor-quality fabric won't hold up, either in sewing or in wear.

Cotton solids or prints, together or separate, make very good quilts. Silks, satins, and velvets make beautiful quilts, but these fabrics are difficult to handle. If this is your first quilting project, stick to cotton. Synthetics do not make good quilts, but you can use blends of cotton and synthetic. Don't use knit fabrics. They tend to stretch and do not make good-looking quilts. Lightweight wools are acceptable. You can also use heavier wools, but the seams will be thicker and the quilt block will be slightly smaller. This won't matter if the entire quilt is made of heavy wools, but it will make a difference when mixing heavy wool with cotton. It's generally best to use all the same kind of fabric in a quilt, but you can successfully combine fabrics of similar texture and appearance, such as polished cotton and satin. If you think there might be a problem, sew up a single quilt block in the fabrics you've chosen before cutting the fabric for the whole quilt.

YARDAGE

The way you color in the quilt design will, of course, determine how much of each color you need. Try to estimate what part of the total colored-in area each color appears to take up. The sewing instructions for each design include a list of pattern pieces for each quilt block and the total number of each piece required for the whole quilt. These totals may help you estimate how much of each color to buy.

The dimensions of the finished quilt are also the measurements for the quilt back. For the back of a 90 × 90-inch quilt you'll need a minimum of two 2½-yard lengths of 45-inch-wide fabric. Adding an extra ½ yard, buy 5½ yards. When estimating the fabric for the quilt top, add another 2 yards to the back yardage, to allow for seams and for waste in cutting. In other words, the total yardage of the colors for the top must add up to at least 7½ yards. If you're going to finish off your quilt with bias seam binding (see Final Assembly, page 26), buy an extra yard of fabric of the color you want for the binding. Remember that these figures are approximations. If you are in doubt, it is better to buy more fabric than less.

CUTTING

Fold the fabric in half, one color at a time, or, if you prefer, fold again so that you can cut through four thicknesses at once. It may be difficult to cut through more than four thicknesses. Take care that the selvages are lined up, and pin the fabric about every 2 feet.

Place the first pattern piece on the fabric. Line up the arrow, if there is one, with the grain line. Arrange a square or oblong piece so that one edge lines up with the grain line.

In quiltmaking, unlike dressmaking, it is not necessary to line up the pieces so that the grain lines all go in the same direction, even for fabrics that have one-way naps, such as velvet or satin. Quilts are more interesting when the shading of different areas varies, and the patterns can be placed in any direction on the fabric as long as the arrows follow the vertical or horizontal grain lines. Examine printed fabrics to determine whether the design is one-way. Most prints look good placed in any direction in a quilt. But if you have a one-way patterned fabric, particularly a stripe, decide how you want to use it in the overall quilt design before cutting.

Using a sharp marking chalk or a felt-tip pen that won't bleed, draw a line, right on the fabric, around the edges of the pattern piece. Repeat this step as many times as necessary until you account for the number required for that piece. For example, if the sewing instructions say you need a total of 52 of the piece you are cutting, and you have folded the fabric in four thicknesses, trace around the pattern piece 13 times. To save fabric and avoid extra marking and cutting, place the pattern piece right up against the cutting line of the piece you have just marked before you trace around the piece again. Finish marking, put a pin through all the layers in the center of each piece marked, and cut.

Beginners may feel more comfortable marking the sewing lines also. Use a tracing wheel and dressmaker's tracing paper, which you can buy at sewing centers or in department stores. Separate the pieces and begin marking. Mark on the wrong side of the fabric. Since quilts have hundreds of pieces and marking them will be tiresome, beginners may soon become as expert as advanced quilters in judging seams and find that they don't have to mark them all.

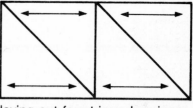

laying out four triangular pieces

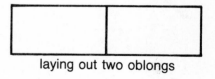

laying out two oblongs

 # STITCHING TECHNIQUES

Many quilters feel that all stitching in a quilt must be done by hand. Others feel that ma-

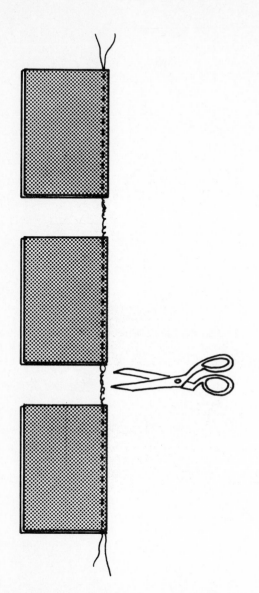

chine stitching is acceptable as long as the final quilting through is done by hand. A few feel that even the final quilting through can be done by machine, but the method described in this book for final quilting involves hand stitching.

The stitching technique that follows describes a quick and efficient way to machine-stitch the pattern pieces together. In this method, the blocks are constructed in assembly-line fashion. You complete each step for all like-numbered pieces. For example, if the instructions say stitch a 1 piece to a 2 piece, stitch *all* the 1 pieces to *all* the 2 pieces before going on to the next step. Run them all through the machine without stopping to backstitch or cut your threads. Run off the end of each piece about 1 inch before starting the next, keeping the presser foot of the machine down. The pieces will be attached to each other by 1-inch threads. When you've sewn all the pieces in that step, lift the presser foot and remove the last piece from the machine. Clip the threads between all the pieces. These twisted threads act as knots that will hold together while these pieces are pressed and stitched into the next pieces.

TURNING CORNERS

It's tricky to turn a corner by hand or machine, but if you follow these instructions slowly and carefully, you'll be able to sew a neat and accurate corner.

The Hexagon and Baby Blocks quilts are sewn entirely by turning corners; there's not a straight seam anywhere. If you're not ready yet for the challenge of sewing quilts made all of turned corners, the instructions that follow will also help you in sewing quilts such as School-house or Tulip, which have only a few corners in each quilt block to turn.

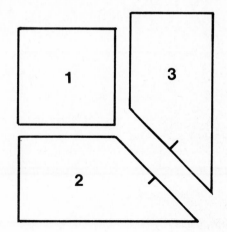

These instructions are based on the typical pattern pieces in the diagram.

Sew 1 to 2. Press seam open.

Sew 3 to 1 and stop at the point indicated by the arrow in the diagram. (This point is at the seamline that joins 1 and 2 and is underneath 3.) Leave the needle down in the fabric. Raise the presser foot and clip the seam right to the needle.

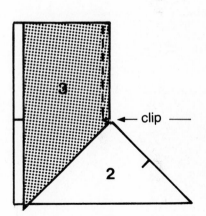

Slide 2 to the left underneath 3 and adjust so that the edge of 2 lines up with the edge of 3 and the notches match. Lower the presser foot and, following the sewing line, stitch right off the end.

Press the seam away from 3.

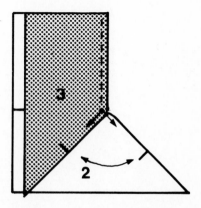

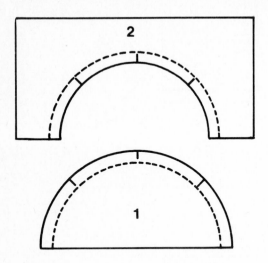

To sew a curved seam, first stay-stitch ¼ inch around the curve on both pieces (1 and 2). Pin the pieces, right sides together, at the notches. Ease 1 into 2 by stretching 2 slightly until the sewing lines line up. Pin often, at right angles to the sewing lines. Hand-baste just inside and very close to the stay-stitching. Make sure the sewing lines match. Remove the pins. Clip both layers right up to but not through the stay-stitching. Machine-stitch over the basting. Remove the basting. Press away from 1.

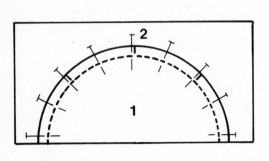

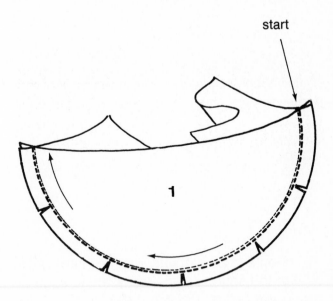

start

The sewing instructions for each quilt tell you to press seams either open or to one side away from the seam line. The quilt block goes together faster if the seams are pressed away from the center of the block, and seams are generally stronger this way. You'll have no choice with curved seams; they can't be pressed open. Press them away from the convex piece (the piece with the outside curve).

Remember that the seam allowance on the patterns in this book is ¼ inch. If you've increased the allowance to ½ inch, you should usually ignore instructions that direct you to press seams open. Press so that the seam allowances are away from the center of the quilt block or away from the side of the seam you are planning to quilt through in the final quilting.

If the fabrics you are using are lightweight, press the seams away from the lighter color whenever possible to keep the darker fabric from showing through.

Press all the pieces in one step before going on to the next step. Always press on the wrong side.

BORDERS

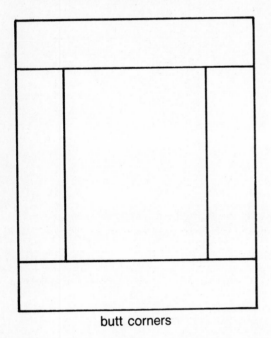

butt corners

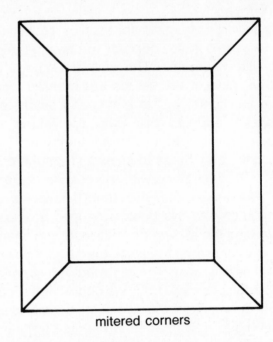

mitered corners

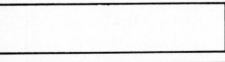

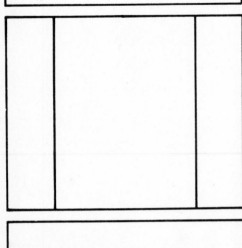

The borders in all the quilt designs have butt corners. They are very easy to sew. Cut out four strips according to the measurements in the sewing instructions. They allow for ¼ inch seam allowance on each side. You'll have two short strips and two long ones. When attaching the borders, always place them right side down onto the face of the quilt. Sew one of the shorter borders down. Sew the other short border to the side opposite. Press seams toward the borders. Sew the two remaining longer borders to the remaining sides.

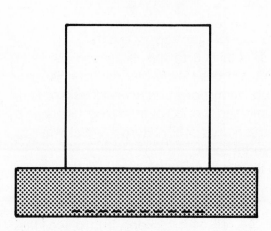

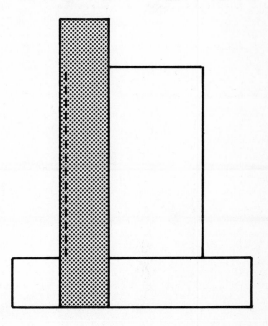

If you'd rather finish the quilt with mitered borders, cut all four border strips the same length, using the measurements for the longer borders. Center one border on one side of the quilt top so that it extends evenly off the ends. Stitch it to ¼ inch from the end of the quilt top. Press away from the quilt top. Repeat with the other three border strips.

Finish the corners one at a time. Arrange so that one strip overlaps another. Fold the border strip that is on top back under itself, making a bias (diagonal) fold between the corner of the quilt top and the outer corner where the two borders meet. Pin, baste, and hand-hem this bias fold down with invisible hem-stitches.

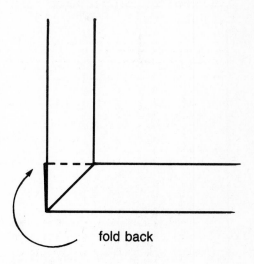

fold back

FINAL ASSEMBLY

After the entire quilt top is finished, the next step is attaching it to the filling and the quilt back. For the quilt filling buy commercial batting, a light, fluffy polyester material sold precut. If you can't find the exact size you need, buy a larger size; it cuts easily. Here are two ways to assemble the quilt.

Method 1. Spread the batting on the floor. Carefully lay the top of the quilt on it, face up, smooth it from the center out, and pin about every 2 feet all over to keep it in place. Machine-stitch ¼ inch from the edges all the way around.

Lay the quilt out on the floor again, batting side on the bottom. Make sure it is smooth and flat, adjusting the pins if necessary. Place the quilt backing right side down on the quilt top and pin the edges every few inches all the way around. Machine-stitch ½ inch from the edges all around, leaving two feet in the middle of one side unstitched. Clip the corners off bluntly, just to the stitching. Pull the quilt right side out through the opening. Push the corners out carefully with the points of a closed scissors. Tuck in the edges of the opening and sew closed with invisible stitching.

Shake the quilt out gently and lay it flat on the floor again. Smooth out carefully, and completely pin again through all the layers, checking often to be sure there are no lumps or bubbles. Hand-baste through all the layers, working from the center out in a grid pattern. Make large basting stitches in rows about six inches apart. Use cotton thread or special quilting thread that

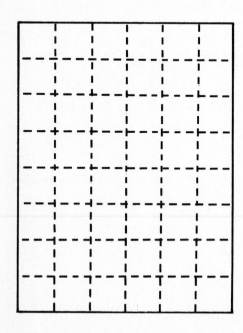

is available in some stores. Don't use polyester thread or cotton thread with a polyester core; it won't pull smoothly through the layers. Use a sharp needle or buy quilting needles. Adjust the pins as you baste, if necessary, to keep the quilt flat. The quilt is now ready to be quilted through.

Method 2. In this second method you'll be constructing a quilt sandwich: quilt back on the bottom, filling in the middle, and quilt top on top. Raw edges are finished off with seam binding.

Place the quilt backing on the floor, right side down, and smooth it out. Lay the batting on the quilt back and put the quilt top, face up, on top of both. Pin all three layers together every six inches or so, checking often to be sure that the layers are smooth and flat on top of each other. Baste through all layers from the center out in a grid pattern of rows about six inches apart, using large basting stitches and cotton or quilting thread. You are now ready to quilt through, as described in the next section.

After quilting through, in Method 2 you must finish off the raw edges with matching or contrasting ½-inch bias seam binding cut from one of the colors used in the quilt. For the seam binding, cut a bias strip 2½ inches wide. This measurement includes ½-inch seam allowances. Cut enough so that the bias strip goes completely around the quilt. Since you won't have a length of fabric long enough to cut a continuous strip, piece it together, following the diagram. Stitch the right side of the bias binding to the top of the quilt ½ inch from the edge. You can start the stitching at the corner or you can place the beginning of the bias strip in the middle of one of the sides. You can sew the strip all around the quilt in one operation, easing the corners, or you can sew separate strips down

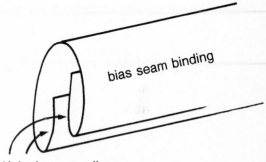

bias seam binding

½ inch seam allowance

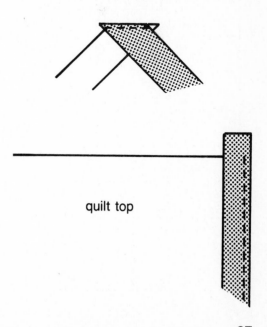

quilt top

each side, tucking in the corners when you've finished. Fold the bias binding over the raw edge so that the edge of the binding just covers the stitches on the quilt bottom. Sew down with invisible stitches.

QUILTING THROUGH

Quilting through is the final stitching that goes through all the layers. It is both functional, keeping all the layers in place, and decorative. Use cotton thread. It's better than polyester thread or thread with a polyester core because it pulls through more smoothly and knots less. Quilting thread, a No. 3 cotton cord, is available in some stores.

Generally, quilters use thread of the same color as the quilt back for this step, but use whatever color you prefer. To cut down on the pulling and knotting, wax the thread with beeswax, readily available in stores. To wax the thread, thread the needle and pull it through the wax ball. For this final quilting use long, thin, sharp needles or quilting needles.

You won't need a quilt frame. The quilt doesn't need to be stretched; you can do the final quilting through as you hold the quilt on your lap. And it's easier to do a continuous running stitch on an unstretched quilt.

In patchwork quilts the quilting-through stitches usually follow the inside shape of the pattern pieces. Commercial batting does not pull apart or lump together, so you need not outline all pieces in stitching. Some quilters prefer a great deal of top quilting and some less.

Decide which pieces you want to outline in stitches and outline the same pieces in each quilt block. Use tiny running stitches, six to ten to the inch, going through all the layers. Stitches look more even if you do several at once in a continuous motion, rather than one at a time. Stitch ¼ inch in from the seam line. Stitches any closer to the seam line will not show up well.

Instead of outlining the pattern pieces, consider tying the layers together. To tie, stitch through all thicknesses at the corners of each quilt block with cotton thread. Using small stitches, stitch over and over again in the same place, much as you'd do if you were sewing on a button. Run the end of the thread under the quilt top and cut off.

Or you can use heavy yarn as a tie. Thread a needle that has a large eye with about two feet of yarn. Sew down from the top and pull the yarn back up through all the layers at the corners of each quilt block or at regular intervals across the quilt top. Cut the yarn so that you have two ends of about equal length and tie in a knot. Leave these ends beyond the knot showing on the top of the quilt. Usually, these yarn ends are about ½ inch, but you can cut them longer if you prefer.

 # ENLARGING A QUILT

You can enlarge any of the quilts in this book by adding rows of quilt blocks to the length or width or to both. Remember, when increasing both length and width, add an extra block to the length for each row of width added. In other words, if the quilt is made up of forty-two blocks, six across and seven down, add six to the length and eight, not seven, to the width to accommodate the new row. Don't forget that the borders, if there are any, will have to be lengthened also.

You can enlarge a quilt just by adding borders to quilts that have none or by increasing given border widths in designs that do have borders. An effective way to do this is to add or widen the borders so that they are as wide as a quilt block. Such wide borders are usually cut out of the fabric of the predominant color of the quilt.

You can also enlarge a quilt with separating strips, if the design does not already call for them. Separating strips are strips at least two inches wide (plus an additional ¼ inch on each side of the strip for seam allowance) inserted between quilt blocks that would otherwise be stitched together. These strips, of course, will change the design as you have colored it in. To see how the quilt will look when assembled, cut out the design from the coloring page. Cut the quilt blocks apart and paste them down on a separate sheet of paper, leaving spaces between them. Then color the spaces between the blocks.

CARE OF QUILTS

Because modern commercial quilt batting is so well made, it is safe to wash a quilt made with it if the quilt fabrics themselves are washable.

Use the cycle for delicate fabrics on your washing machine. The batting won't ball up inside. But dry cleaning is a gentler way to clean a quilt. After so much work, any protective measure is a good idea, so dry cleaning is recommended over washing. Hang out the quilt for a few days to get rid of the smell of the cleaning fluid.

Two versions of the Pineapple design

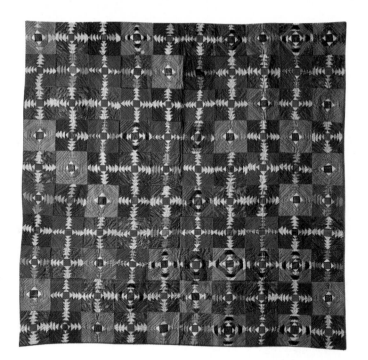

Church Steps, made of silk and wool, c. 1890

Pineapple Log Cabin, made of cotton, c. 1870

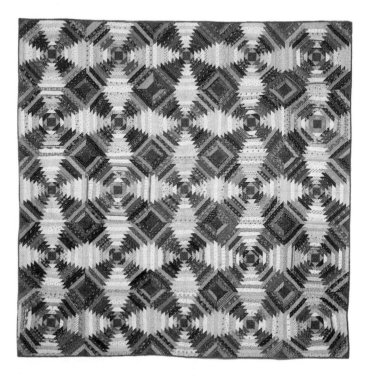

All photographs courtesy of America Hurrah Antiques, New York City

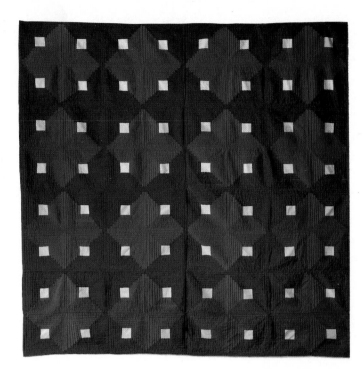

Three versions of the Log Cabin design (also called Court House Steps design)

Mennonite Log Cabin, made of cotton, c. 1890

Barn Raising Log Cabin, made of cotton, c. 1890

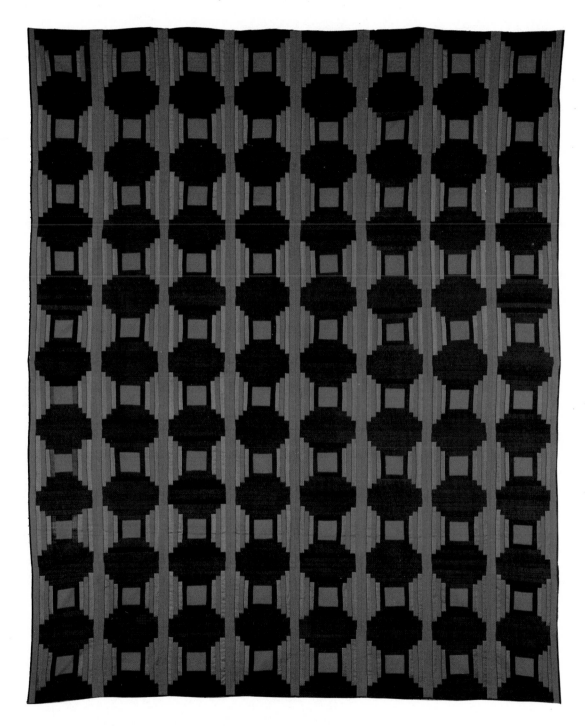

Mennonite Court House Steps, made of wool challis, c. 1910

Two versions of the Hexagon design

Mosaic Star, made of cotton, c. 1850

Mosaic, made of cotton and chintz, c. 1840

THE QUILT DESIGNS

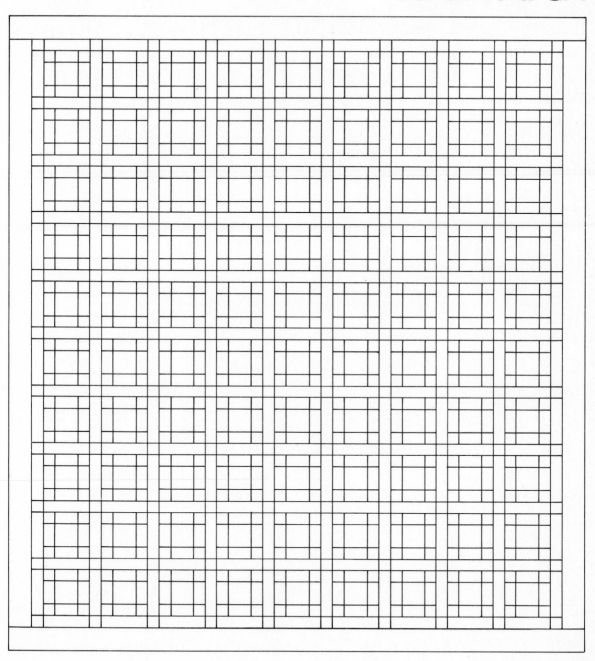

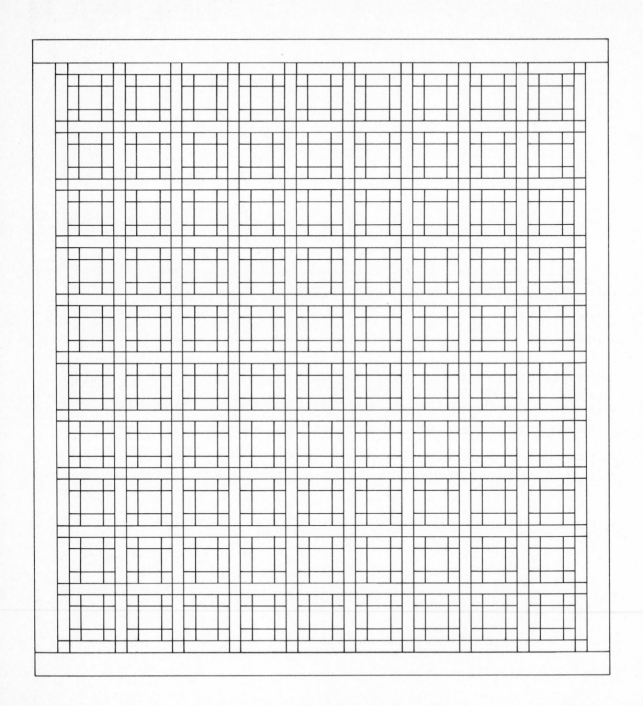

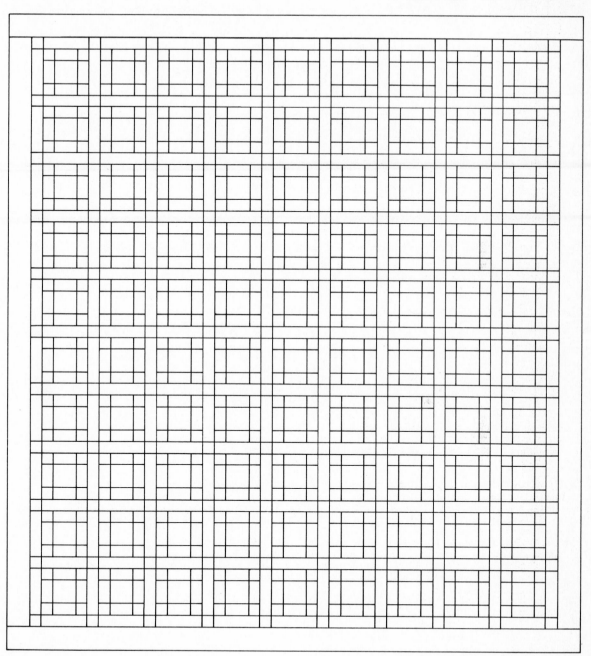

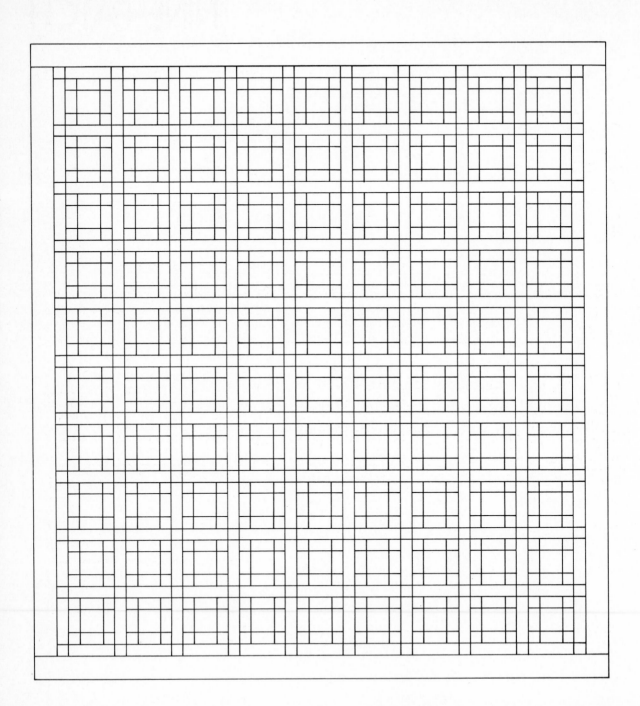

NINE-PATCH

This is a very easy quilt to make. It is ideal for a beginner.

The finished quilt measures 100 × 110 inches, including borders.

There are ninety 10-inch blocks.

Pattern piece	In quilt	In each block
1	90	1
2	360	4
3	470	5
4	199	2

Nineteen of the 4 pieces and twenty of the 3 pieces are not part of the quilt block as it is assembled according to the instructions given here. They make up the right and bottom edges of the quilt top and are sewn to the proper places after the blocks are assembled.

Cut two border pieces 4½ × 100½ inches and two pieces 4½ × 102½ inches.

Sew a 2 to one side of each 1. Sew a 2 to the opposite side of each 1. Press seams open.

Sew a 3 to one end of each remaining 2. Sew a 3 to the other end. Press seams open.

Sew a 3-2-3 section to the top of each 2-1-2 section. Sew a 3-2-3 section to the bottom of each 2-1-2 section. Press seams open.

3	4

4	3	2	3
	2	1	2
	3	2	3

Sew a 4 to the left side of each block just completed. Press seams open.

Sew a 3 to one end of each remaining 4. Press seams open.

Sew a 3-4 section to the top of the 1-2-3-4 block. Repeat for each block. Press seams open.

Sew nine blocks together to form one horizontal row. Be sure the 4 pieces always lie on the top and the left side with a 3 between them. Repeat for a total of ten rows.

On the right side of each row sew a 3-4 section so that the 3 is placed in the upper right corner. Press seams open. Sew the ten rows together to form the quilt top. Press seams open.

Sew the remaining 3-4 sections together end to end so they form a row of alternating 3 and 4 pieces. Sew the remaining 3 on the end next to a 4. Press seams open. Sew this row to the bottom of the quilt, sewing 3 pieces to the ends of 4 pieces. Be sure to match seams at intersections.

Sew the two 4½- × 102½-inch borders to opposite sides of the quilt top. Press seams toward borders. Sew the two 4½- × 100½-inch borders to the top and bottom. Press seams toward borders.

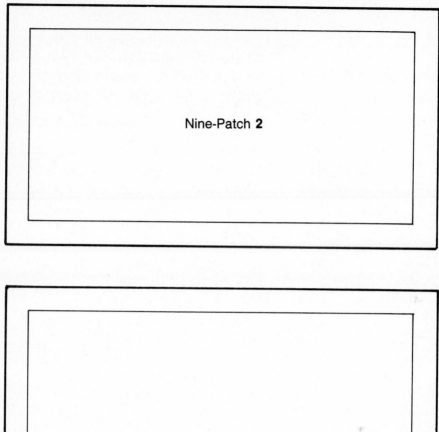

Nine-Patch **2**

Nine-Patch **1**

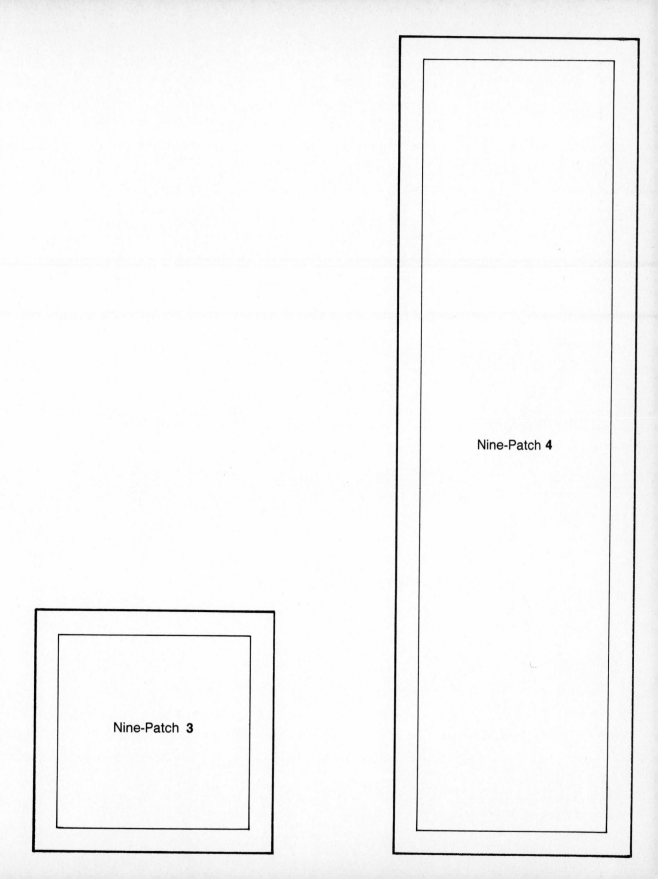

Nine-Patch **4**

Nine-Patch **3**

46

JACK-IN-THE-BOX

Although the design looks complicated, this is an easy quilt to assemble. Care must be taken in sewing to match seams at intersections.

The finished quilt measures 74 × 86 inches, including borders.

There are forty-two 10-inch blocks.

Pattern piece	In quilt	In each block
1	168	4
2	672	16
3	168	4
4	168	4
5	72	1
6	71	

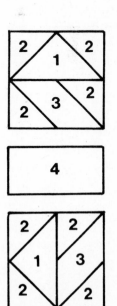

Cut two border pieces 2½ × 74½ inches and two 2½ × 82½ inches.

Sew a 2 to one notched side of each 3, matching notches. Repeat for the other bias side of each 3. Press seams open.

Sew a 2 to one bias side of each 3, matching notches. Repeat for the other bias side of each 3. Press seams open.

Sew a 2-1-2 section to each 2-3-2 section. Press seams open.

Sew a 4 to the 2-3-2 part of eighty-four of the 1-2-3 sections just completed. Sew the remaining sections to the other side of each 4, with the 3 pieces going in the other direction. Press seams toward 4.

Sew a 4 to each 5. Sew another 4 to the other side of each 5. Press seams open.

Sew these 4-5-4 sections between the completed 1-2-3-4 sections, checking diagram of the quilt block to be sure the 1 pieces are pointing in the proper direction. Match the seams that intersect. Press seams open.

Sew a 6 to the right side of thirty-five blocks. Sew five of these blocks together in a horizontal row so that a 6 separates each block. Sew a block on the right end of the row next to the 6. Repeat for a total of seven rows of blocks. Press seams toward 6.

Sew a 5 to the short side of each remaining 6. Sew five 5-6 sections together end to end, to form a strip of alternating 5 and 6 pieces. Sew a 6 to the end next to the 5. Repeat for a total of six strips. Sew these strips between each row of blocks, matching seams at intersections.

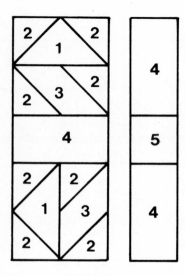

Sew the two 2½- × 82½-inch borders to each side of the quilt top. Press seams toward borders. Sew the two 2½- × 74½-inch borders to the top and bottom. Press seams toward borders.

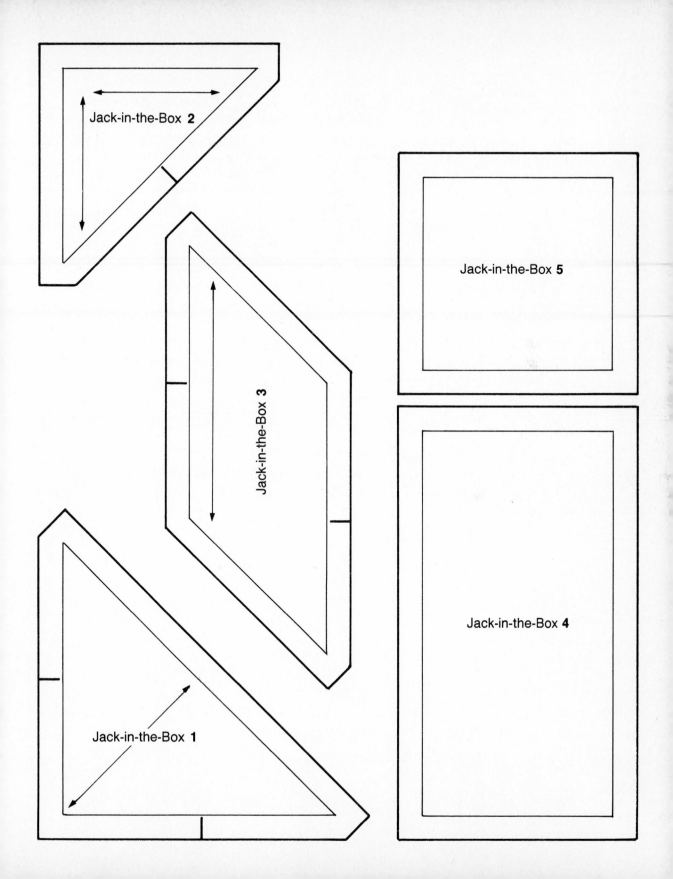

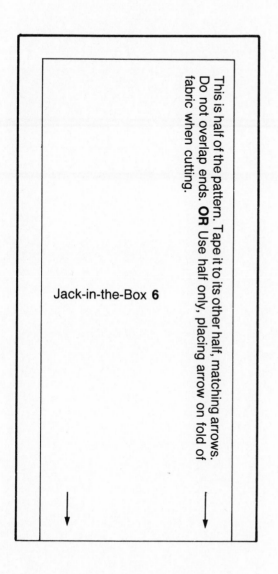

This is half of the pattern. Tape it to its other half, matching arrows. Do not overlap ends. **OR** Use half only, placing arrow on fold of fabric when cutting.

Jack-in-the-Box **6**

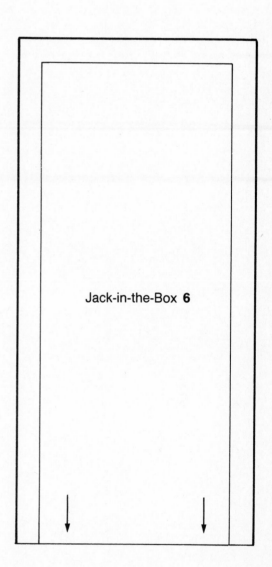

Jack-in-the-Box **6**

ECCENTRIC STAR

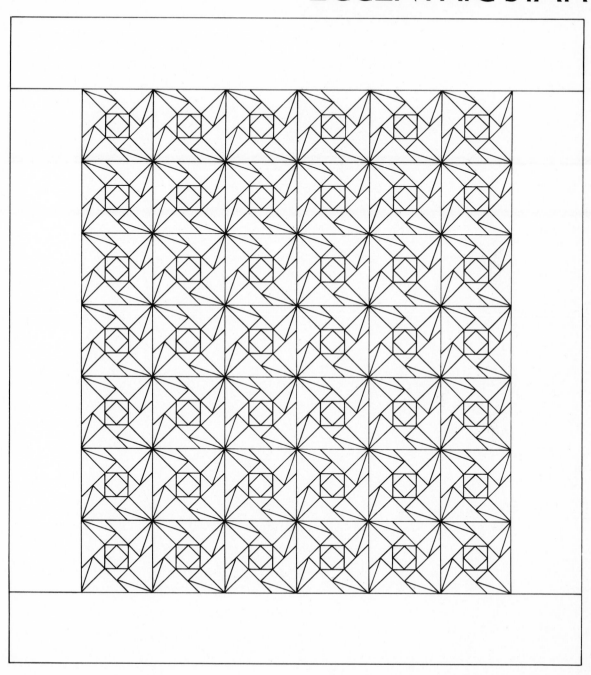

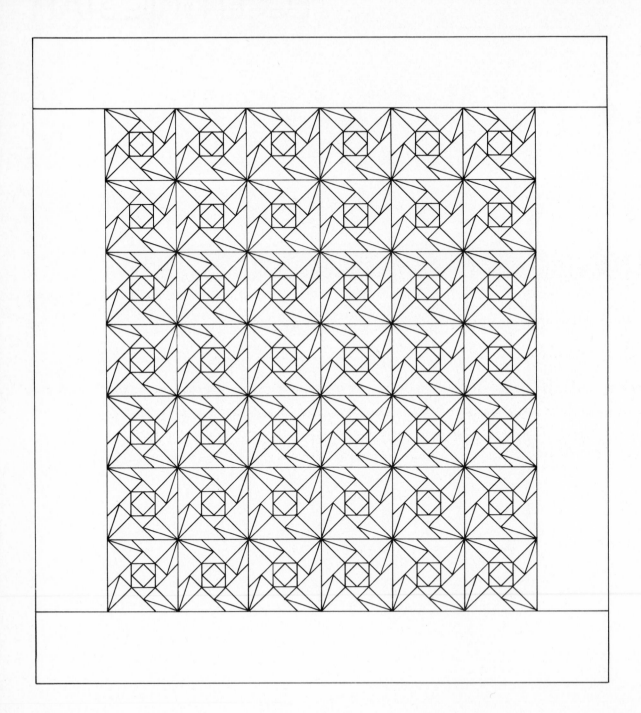

ECCENTRIC STAR

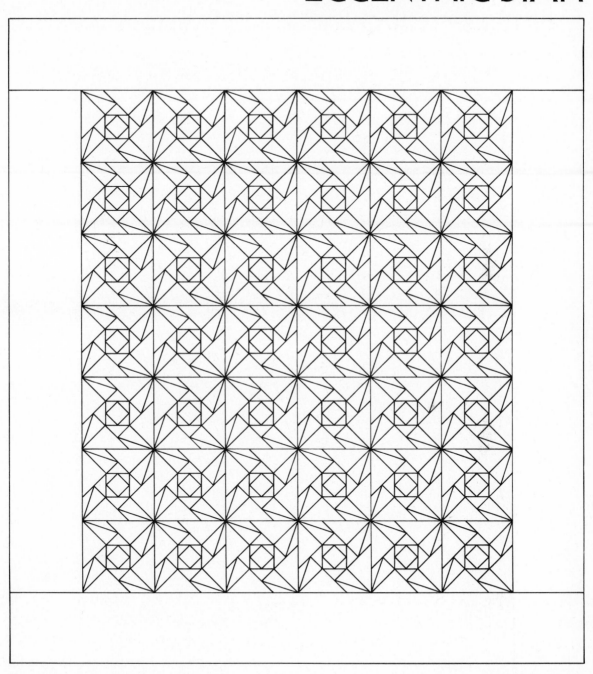

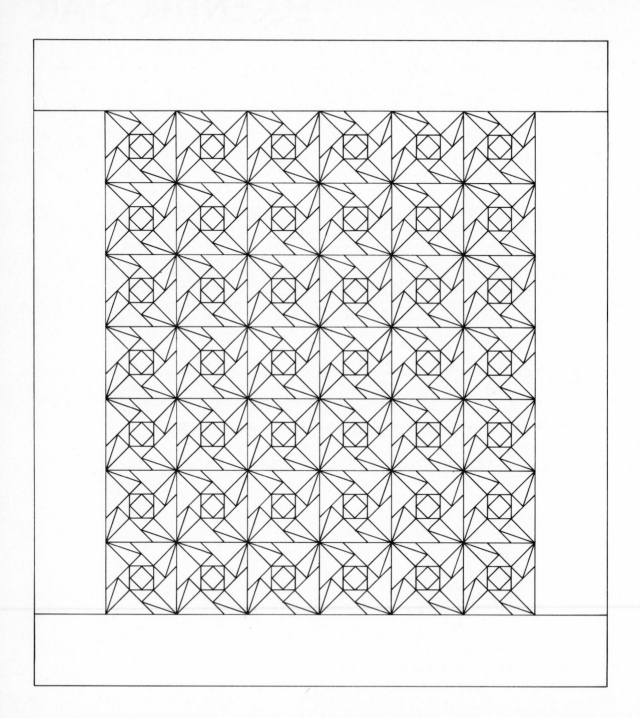

ECCENTRIC STAR

This quilt looks a lot more difficult to sew than it really is. Make sure to check the arrangement of the pattern pieces as you work.

The finished quilt measures 72 × 81 inches.

There are forty-two 9-inch blocks.

Pattern piece	In quilt	In each block
1	42	1
2	168	4
3	168	4
4	168	4
5	168	4
6	168	4

Cut two border pieces 9½ × 63½ inches and two pieces 9½ × 72½ inches. Be sure to cut pattern pieces 4, 5, and 6 all right side up on right side of fabric so that they will face in the same direction when sewn into the blocks.

Sew a 2 to one side of each 1, matching notches. Sew a 2 to the opposite side of each 1. Press seams open.

Repeat for the other two sides.

Sew a 3 to one side of each of the 1-2 sections just completed. Sew a 3 to the opposite side. Press seams open.

Repeat for the other two sides.

Sew a 4 to all the 5 pieces, matching notches. Press seams open.

Sew a 6 to all the 5 pieces in the 4-5 sections just completed, matching notches. Press seams open.

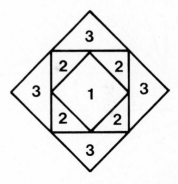

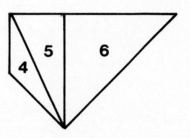

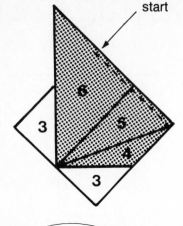

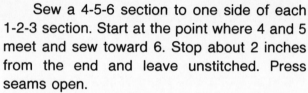

start

Sew a 4-5-6 section to one side of each 1-2-3 section. Start at the point where 4 and 5 meet and sew toward 6. Stop about 2 inches from the end and leave unstitched. Press seams open.

Sew a 4-5-6 section to each 1-2-3 section to the left of the 4-5-6 section just completed. Sew right off both ends; that is, complete the seam. Press seams open.

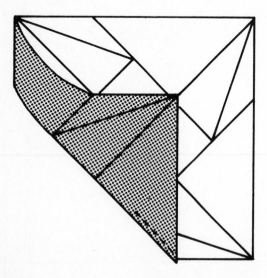

Working clockwise, sew a 4-5-6 section to the remaining two sides of each 1-2-3 section. Press seams open.

To finish off the seam that was left un-stitched in the first 4-5-6 section, pick it up where it was left open and continue right off the end, taking in the side of the last 4-5-6 section. Press seams open.

Sew six blocks together to form one horizontal row of blocks. Repeat for a total of seven rows. Press seams open.

Sew these rows together, matching seams at intersections. Press seams open.

Sew the two 63½-inch borders to both sides of the quilt top. Press seams toward borders. Sew the two 72½-inch borders to the top and bottom. Press seams toward borders.

60

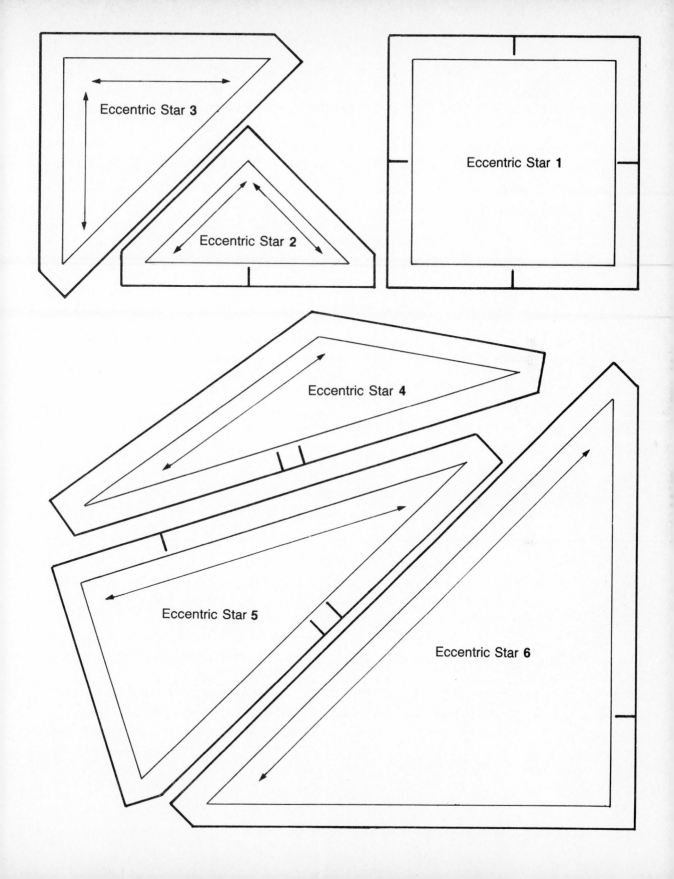

BOW TIE

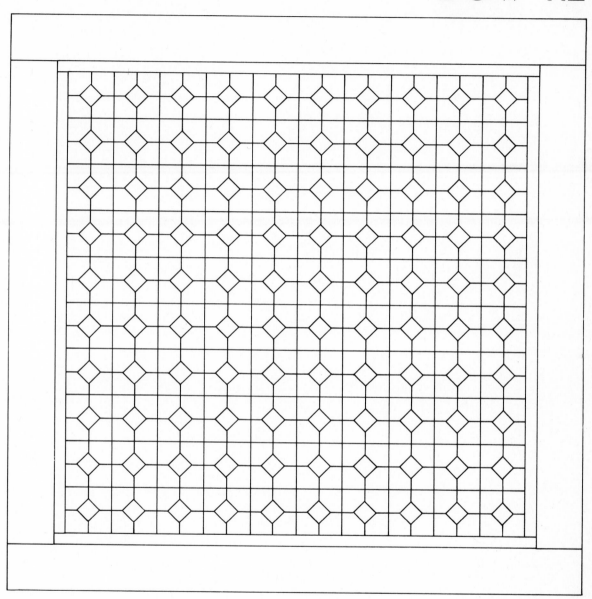

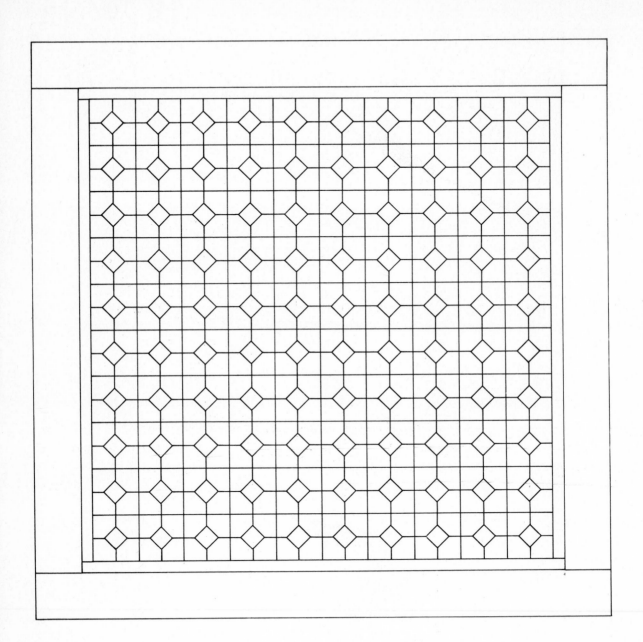

BOW TIE

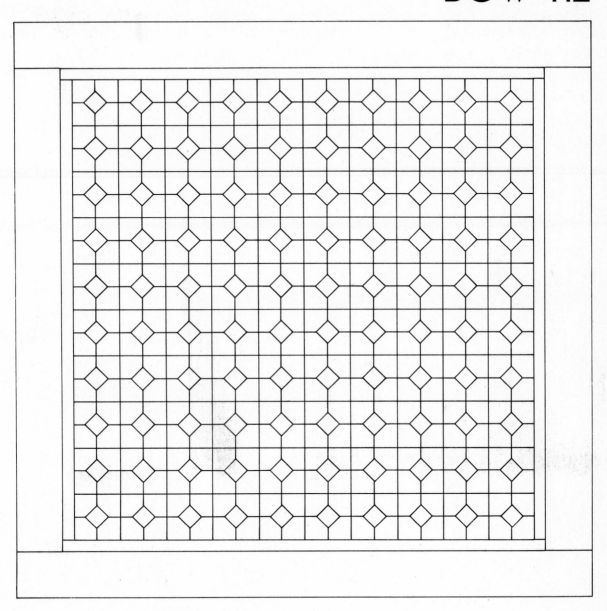

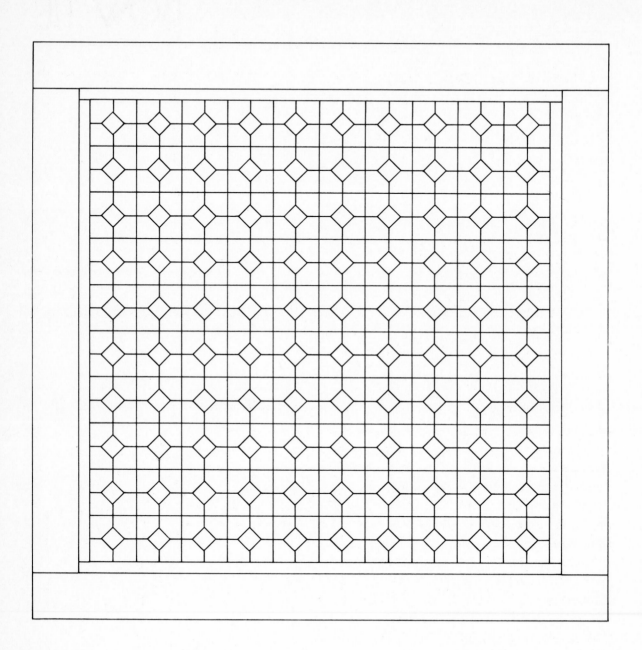

BOW TIE

This is not an easy quilt for the beginner because of the number of corners that have to be turned.

The finished quilt measures 75 × 75 inches including borders.

There are one hundred 6-inch blocks.

Pattern piece	In quilt	In each block
1	100	1
2	400	4

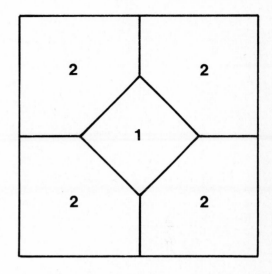

For the inside border cut two 2- × 60½-inch strips and two 2- × 63½-inch strips. For the outside border cut two 6½- × 63½-inch strips and two 6½- × 75½-inch strips.

Sew a 2 to one side of each 1, matching notches. Press seams toward 2.

Sew a 2 to the right side of each section just completed. Begin at the corner of 1 and stitch toward the already attached 2. Clip to the needle, turn the corner, and stitch the two 2 pieces together. (For instructions in turning corners see page 20.) Press the seams between the 1 and 2 pieces toward 2 and the seams between the 2 pieces open. Repeat until each 1 piece is surrounded by four 2 pieces.

Sew ten blocks together to form one row. Repeat nine times, for a total of ten rows. Press seams open. Sew the ten rows together, matching the seams at the intersections to form the quilt top. Press seams open.

Sew the two 2- × 60½-inch borders to

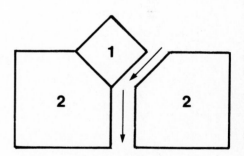

opposite sides of the quilt top. Press seams toward borders. Sew the two 2- × 63½-inch borders to the top and bottom. Press seams toward borders.

Sew the two 6½- × 63½-inch borders to opposite sides of the quilt top. Press seams toward borders. Sew the two 6½- × 75½-inch borders to the top and bottom. Press seams toward borders.

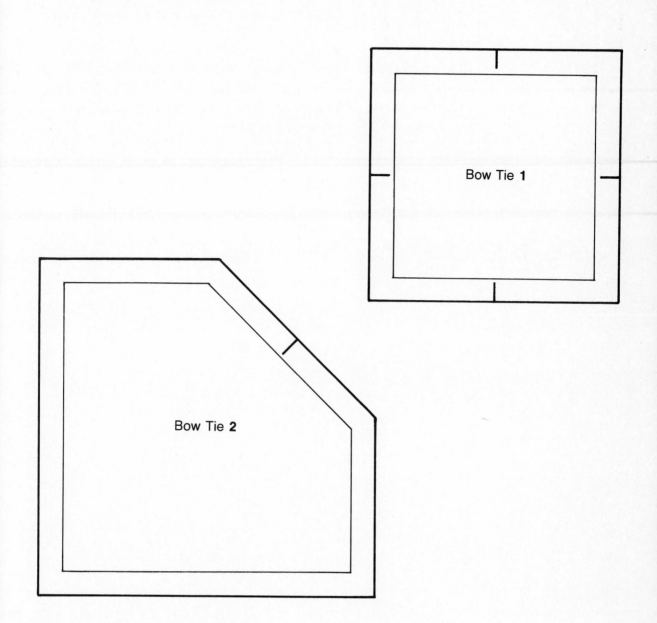

Bow Tie **1**

Bow Tie **2**

SCHOOLHOUSE

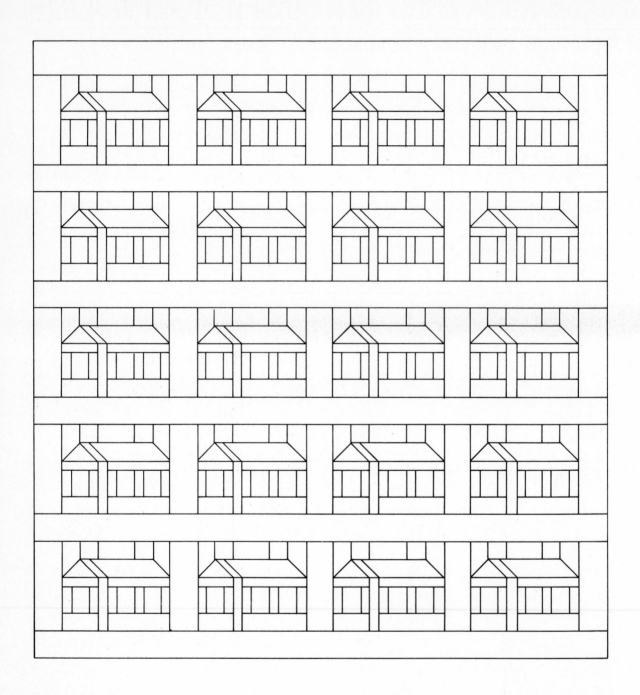

72

SCHOOLHOUSE

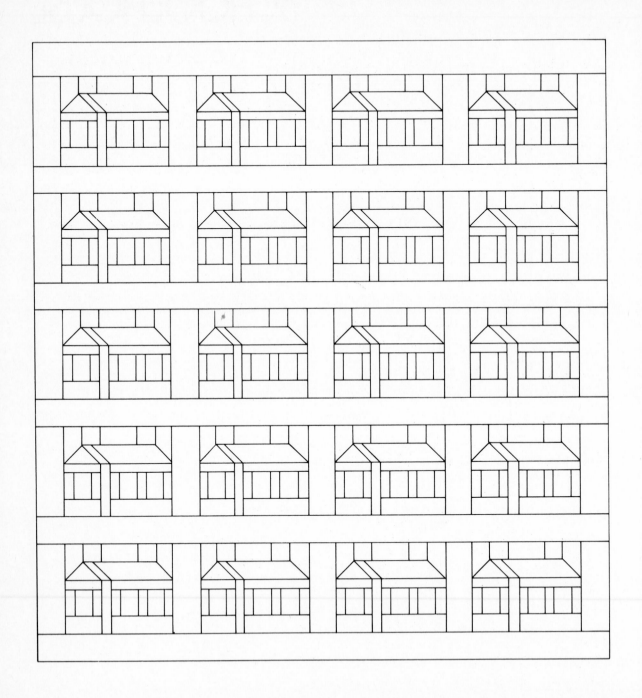

SCHOOLHOUSE

Although there are two corners to be turned in each square, this is not a difficult quilt to assemble.

The finished quilt, including 3-inch borders, measures 63 × 68 inches.

There are twenty 10- × 12-inch blocks.

Pattern piece	In quilt	In each block
1	60	3
2	100	5
3	20	1
4	20	1
5	20	1
6	20	1
7	20	1
8	20	1
9	20	1
10	20	1
11	40	2
12	20	1
13	40	2
14	25	

Cut six separating strips 3½ × 63½ inches. Cut piece 13 on fabric folded right sides together so that, when cut, half are mirror images of the other half.

Sew the 1 and 2 pieces together down their long sides. Forty 2 pieces will be left over. Set aside. Sew forty of the 1-2 sections together with a 1 always next to a 2. The result will be twenty 2-1-2-1 sections.

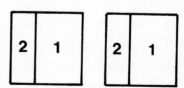

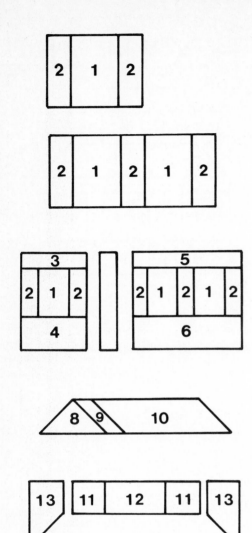

Sew a 2 to the 1 on the end of each 2-1 and 2-1-2-1 sections. Press seams open.

Sew a 3 on top of each 2-1-2 section. Sew a 4 on the bottom. Press both seams away from the 2-1-2 sections.

Sew a 5 on top of each 2-1-2-1-2 section and a 6 on the bottom. Press both seams away from the 2-1-2-1-2 sections.

Sew a 7 down the middle of both sections just completed so the 2-1-2 sections end up on the left side and the 2-1-2-1-2 on the right. Repeat for each block. Press seams open.

Sew an 8 to each 9, matching notches. Press seams open.

Sew a 10 to each 9, matching notches. Press seams open.

Sew an 11 to one side of each 12. Sew an 11 to the other side of each 12. Press seams open.

Sew an 11-12-11 section to the top of each 8-9-10 section. Press seams open.

Sew a 13 to the outside edge of each 11, turning the corners at 8 and 10 to finish. (For instructions in turning corners see page 20.) Press seams away from 13.

Sew the top section of each schoolhouse (roof) to the bottom (house). Press seams open.

Sew a 14 to the left side of each block. Sew four blocks together side by side so that they form a horizontal row of blocks. Repeat for a total of five rows. Sew a 14 to the right end of each row. Press seams toward 14. There are now five horizontal rows of four blocks.

Sew the separating strips between these rows and on the top and bottom to form quilt top. Press seams toward strips.

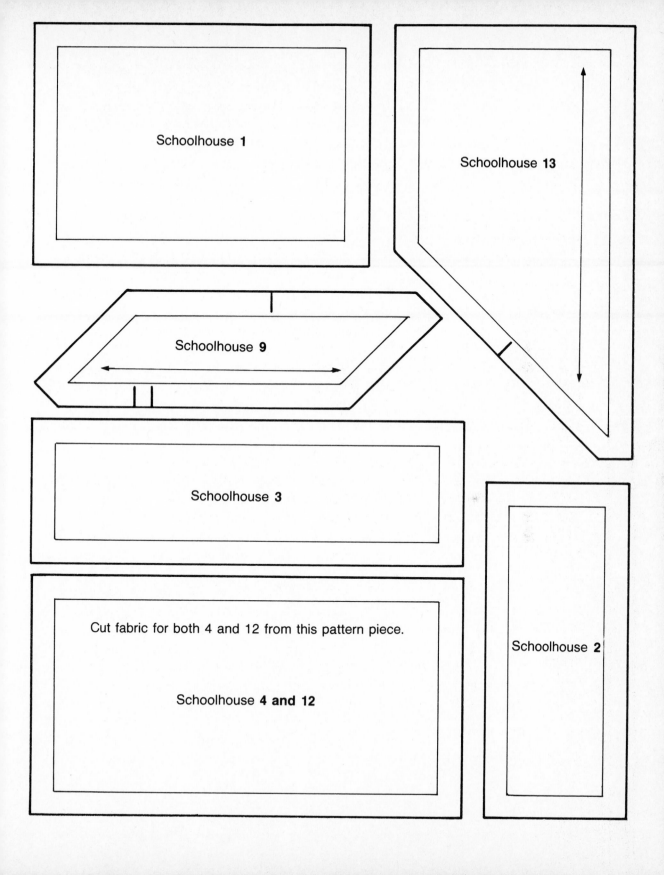

Schoolhouse **1**

Schoolhouse **13**

Schoolhouse **9**

Schoolhouse **3**

Cut fabric for both 4 and 12 from this pattern piece.

Schoolhouse **4 and 12**

Schoolhouse **2**

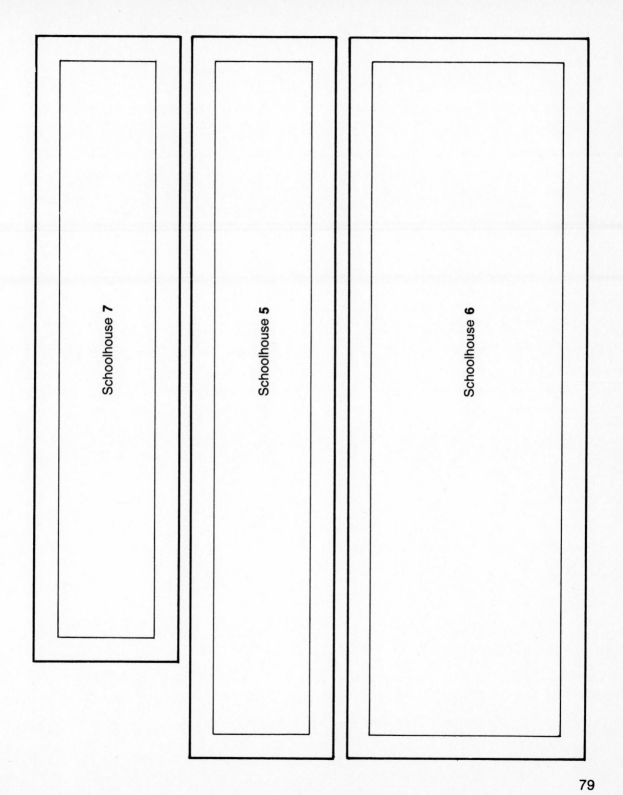

Schoolhouse 7

Schoolhouse 5

Schoolhouse 6

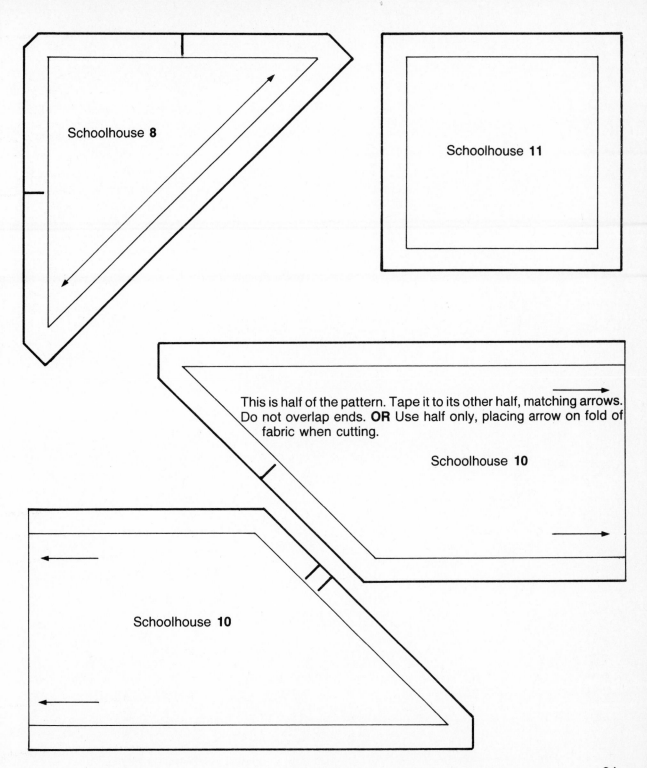

Schoolhouse **8**

Schoolhouse **11**

This is half of the pattern. Tape it to its other half, matching arrows. Do not overlap ends. **OR** Use half only, placing arrow on fold of fabric when cutting.

Schoolhouse **10**

Schoolhouse **10**

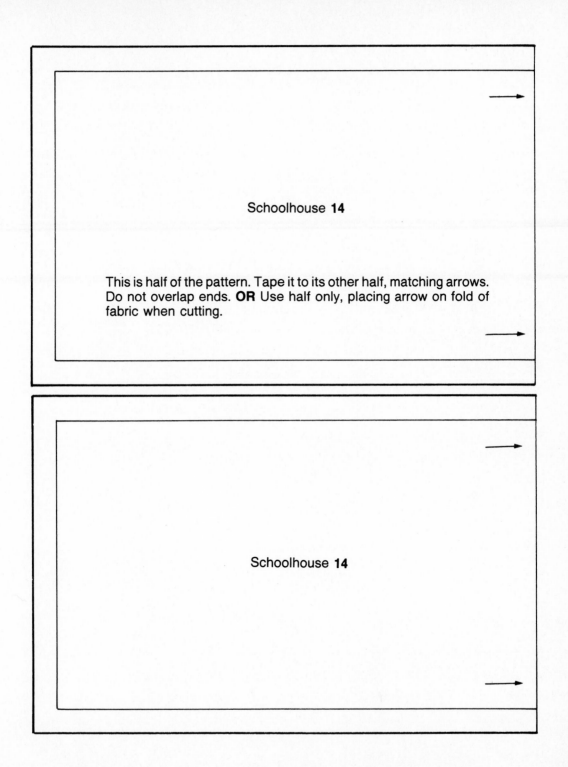

Schoolhouse **14**

This is half of the pattern. Tape it to its other half, matching arrows. Do not overlap ends. **OR** Use half only, placing arrow on fold of fabric when cutting.

Schoolhouse **14**

MORNING STAR

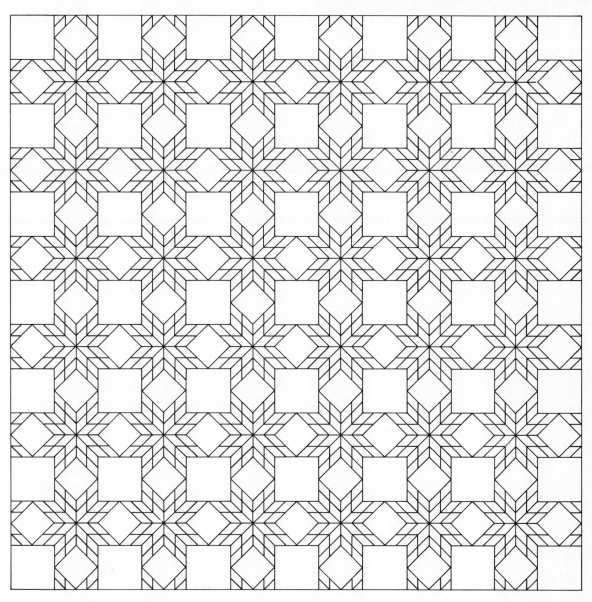

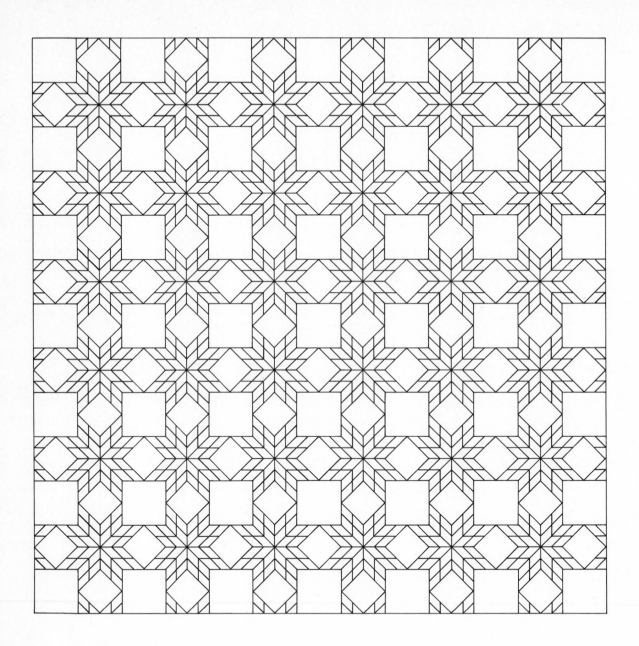

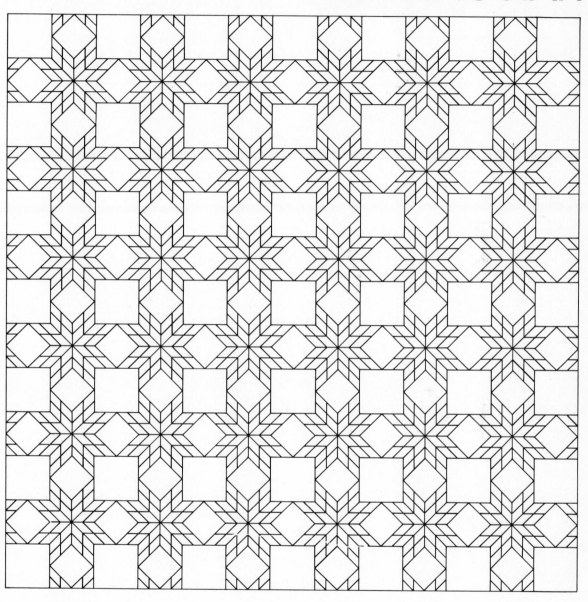

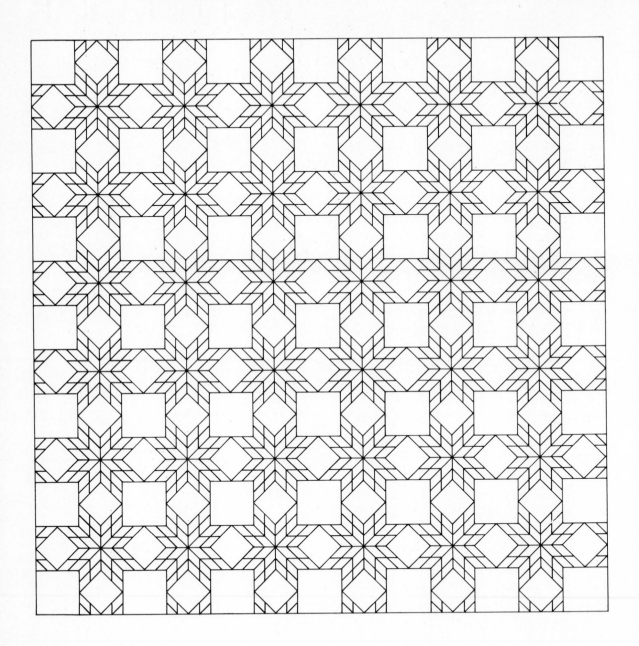

88

MORNING STAR

This quilt may be difficult for beginners to sew. There are many corners to be turned, and the assembly is tricky.

The finished quilt measures 74¾ × 74¾ inches.

There are eighty-four 5¾- × 11½-inch blocks and forty-nine squares.

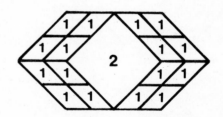

Pattern piece	In quilt	In each block
1	1344	16
2	84	1
3	49	

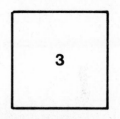

Half the 1 pieces are mirror images of the other half. Cut them on fabric folded right sides together, but study the colored-in design carefully before cutting and sewing pieces or sections together. The quilt is assembled by sewing six blocks into seven vertical rows, alternating with the squares. The other blocks are turned at right angles and are sewn to the completed rows. Read all the instructions and study the diagrams before sewing.

Sew all the 1 pieces together in groups of two. Press seams open.

Sew these 1-1 sections together in groups of two, matching seams at the intersections. Be sure to check your color scheme before sewing, to make sure that you will be able to assemble the pieces in their proper place in the next step.

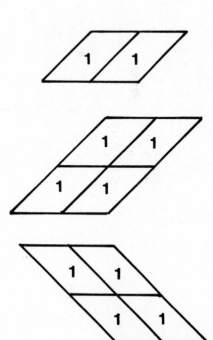

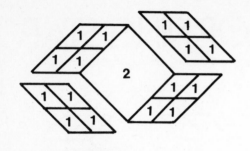
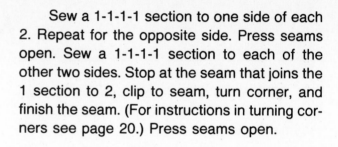

Sew a 1-1-1-1 section to one side of each 2. Repeat for the opposite side. Press seams open. Sew a 1-1-1-1 section to each of the other two sides. Stop at the seam that joins the 1 section to 2, clip to seam, turn corner, and finish the seam. (For instructions in turning corners see page 20.) Press seams open.

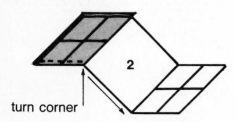

turn corner

Sew six of the blocks just completed to seven 3 pieces, creating a vertical row beginning and ending with a 3 piece, alternating the blocks and squares. Repeat for a total of seven rows. Press seams open.

Turn the remaining 1-2 blocks on their sides and sew to the right side of each 3 in one of the vertical rows. Turn corners at the seams that join the blocks to the 3 pieces. Press seams open. Repeat for a total of 6 rows.

Sew the 6 rows together to form the quilt top. Sew the remaining row of 1-2 and 3 sections to the right outside edge.

Trim off the points of the blocks on the outside edges flush with the 3 pieces.

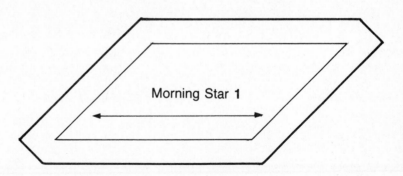

Morning Star **1**

Morning Star **2**

Morning Star **3**

FENCE RAIL, OR JACOB'S LADDER

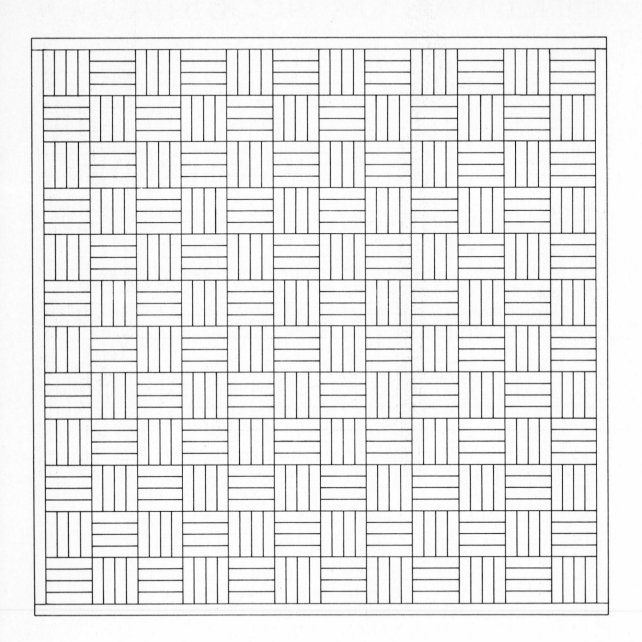

96

FENCE RAIL, OR JACOB'S LADDER

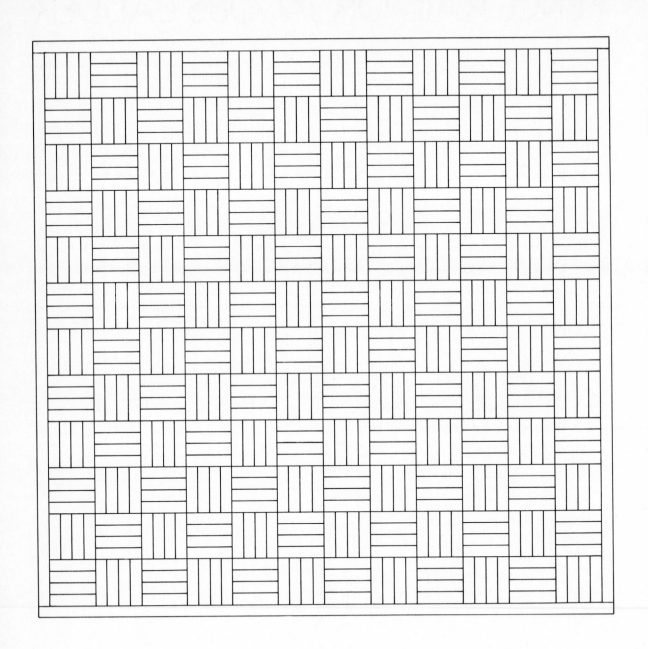

98

FENCE RAIL, OR JACOB'S LADDER

This is one of the easiest quilts to make.

The finished quilt measures 100 × 100 inches, including borders.

There are 144 8-inch blocks.

Pattern piece	In quilt	In each block
1	576	4

Cut two 2½- × 96½-inch and two 2½- × 100½-inch border pieces.

Sew pieces and blocks together according to your color scheme. For faster cutting and sewing, use the following instructions:

Cut a cardboard pattern 2½ inches wide and as long as the width of the fabric. For example, if your fabric is 44 inches wide, the pattern piece will be 2½ × 44 inches.

Lay out the fabric in double or quadruple layers, folding along the width. Match and pin the selvages.

Lay the pattern across the width of the fabric and mark every 2½ inches with a sharp chalk or felt-tip pen. Pin through the center of each 2½-inch section and cut.

Sew four strips together according to your color scheme. Press seams open. Cut into 8½-inch blocks.

On the floor, arrange the blocks according to the color scheme, alternating the direction of the stripes.

Sew twelve blocks together to form one horizontal row. Repeat for a total of twelve rows. Press seams open.

Sew the twelve rows together to form the quilt top. Press seams open.

Sew the two 2½- × 100½-inch borders to opposite sides of the quilt top. Press seams toward borders.

Sew the two 2½- × 96½-inch borders to the top and bottom. Press seams toward borders.

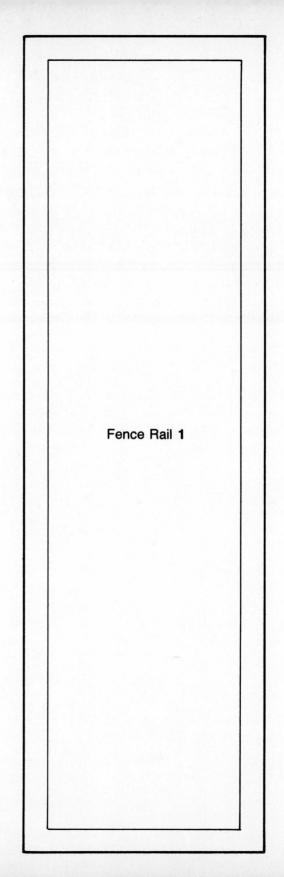

Fence Rail **1**

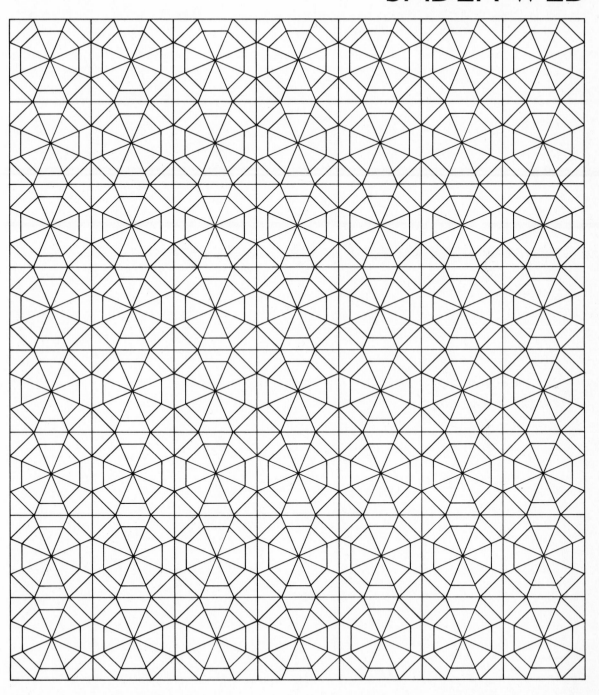

104

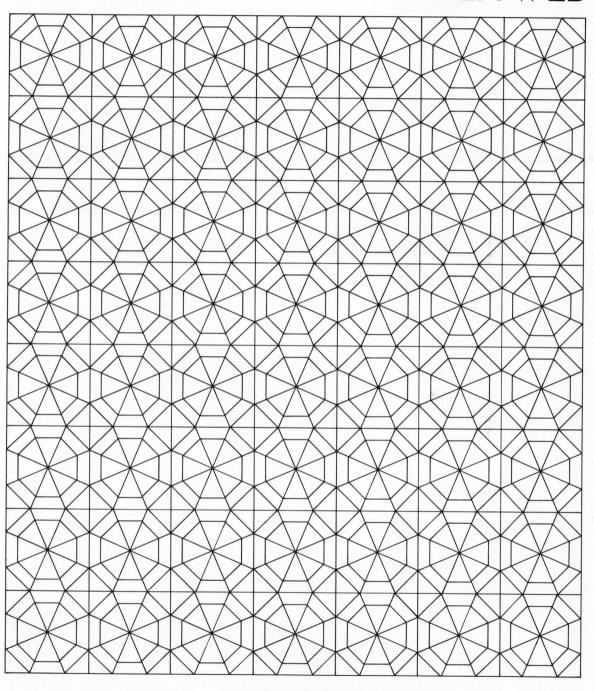

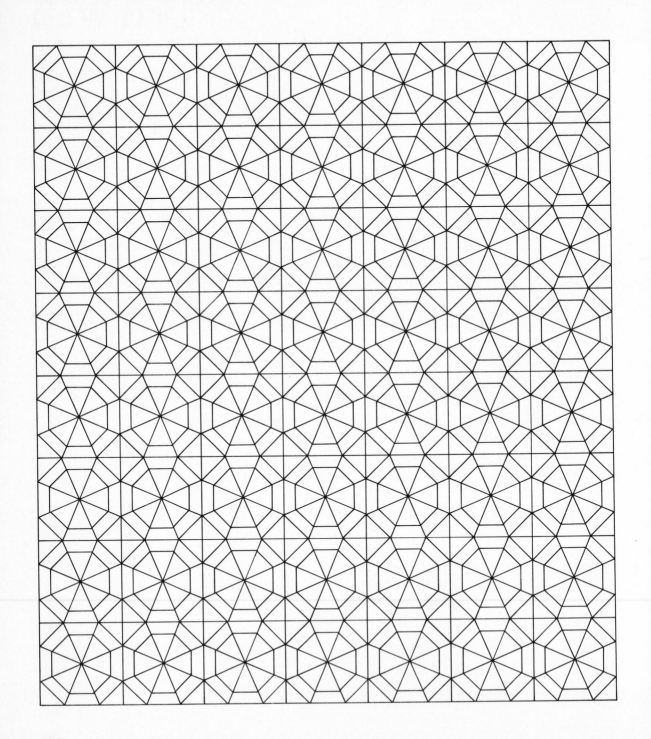

106

SPIDER WEB

This quilt is easy to make.

The finished quilt measures 70 × 80 inches.

There are fifty-six 10-inch blocks.

Pattern piece	In quilt	In each block
1	448	8
2	448	8
3	224	4

Sew all the 1 pieces to the 2 pieces matching notches. Press seams open.

Sew two 1-2 sections together. Press seams open.

Sew the sections just completed together to form half circles, taking care that the seams meet in the center. Press seams open.

Sew the halves together, matching seams at the intersections. Press seams open.

Sew a 3 to every other 2 on each block, matching notches. Press seams open.

Sew seven blocks together to form one horizontal row of blocks. Repeat seven times, for a total of eight rows. Press seams open.

Sew the rows of blocks together to form the quilt top, matching the seams at the intersections. Press seams open.

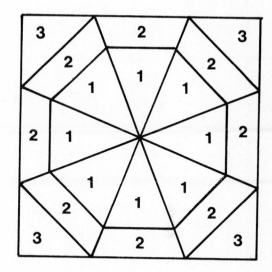

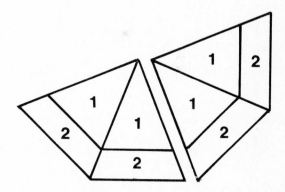

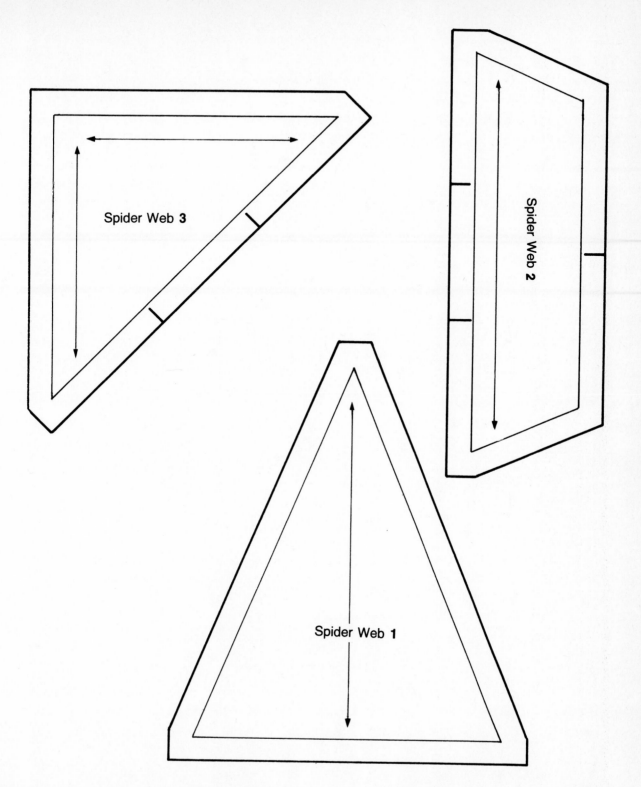

Spider Web **3**

Spider Web **2**

Spider Web **1**

FISH BLOCK

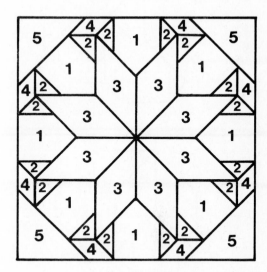

Because there are many corners to be turned in this quilt, it may be difficult for the beginner.

The finished quilt measures 72 × 84 inches.

There are forty-two 12-inch blocks.

Pattern piece	In quilt	In each block
1	336	8
2	672	16
3	336	8
4	336	8
5	168	4

Sew a 2 to one side of each 1, matching double notches. Sew a 2 to the opposite side of each 1. Press seams open.

Sew a 3 to the left side of each 1-2 section just completed, matching notches. Press seams open.

Lay out eight 1-2-3 sections right side up, according to the diagram of the quilt block, and observe how they fan out from the center. Join two 1-2-3 sections. Start by sewing the 3 pieces together, matching notches. Stop at the seam where 3 joins 1. Clip to seam, turn corner, and finish off the seam that joins 3 to 1 and 2. (For instructions in turning corners, see page 20.) Repeat until all 1-2-3 sections are joined together in groups of two. Press seams open.

Sew together the sections just completed in groups of two to form half blocks. Be sure the seams between the 3 pieces come together neatly in the center. Press seams open.

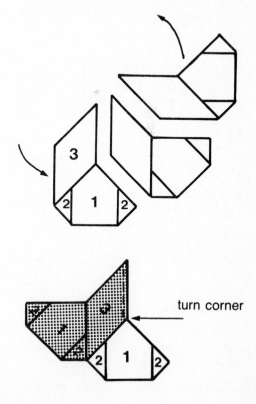

turn corner

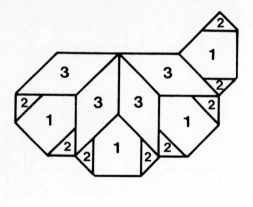

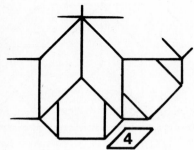

Join the halves together, carefully matching the seams in the center. Press seams open.

Sew a 4 between the 2 pieces. Turn the corner at the seam where the 2 pieces meet. Press seams away from 4.

Sew a 5 to each of the four corners of each block. Press seams open.

Sew six blocks together to form one horizontal row. Repeat for a total of seven rows. Press seams open.

Sew the seven rows together to form the quilt top. Press seams open.

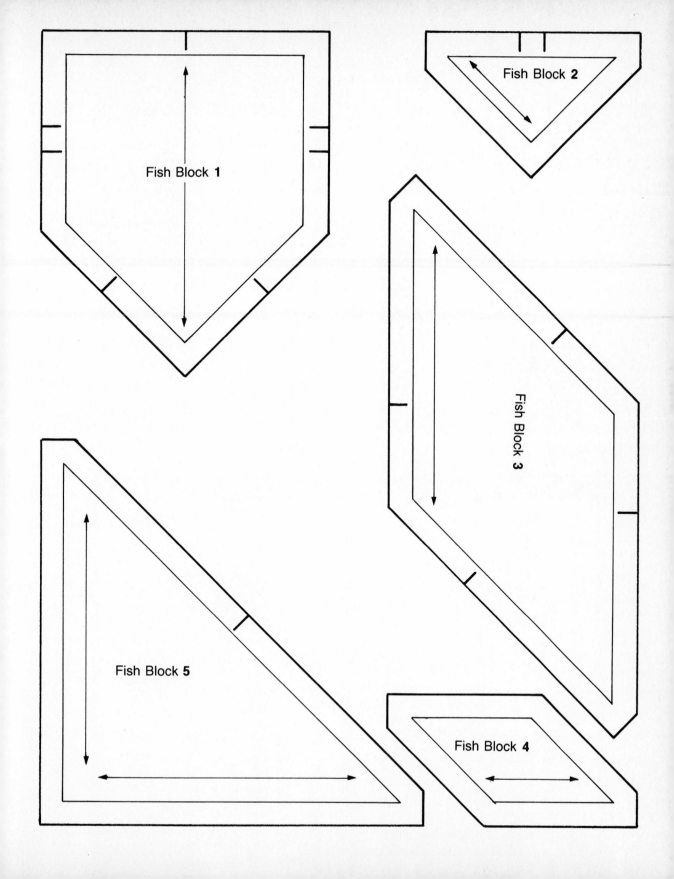

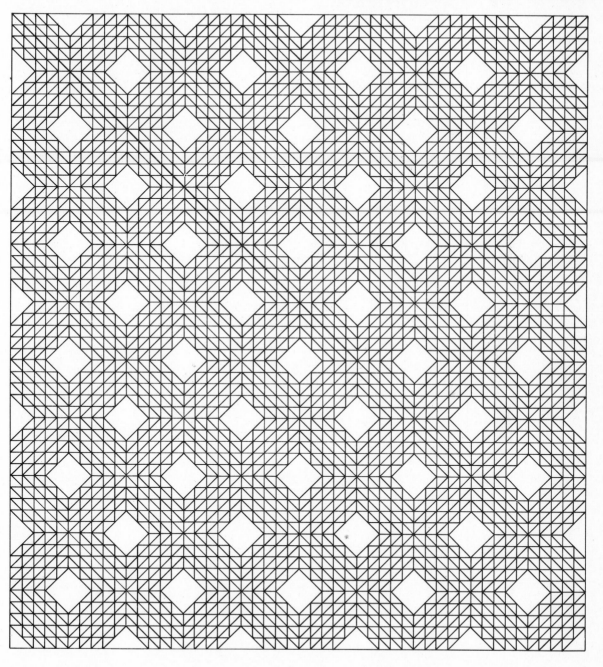

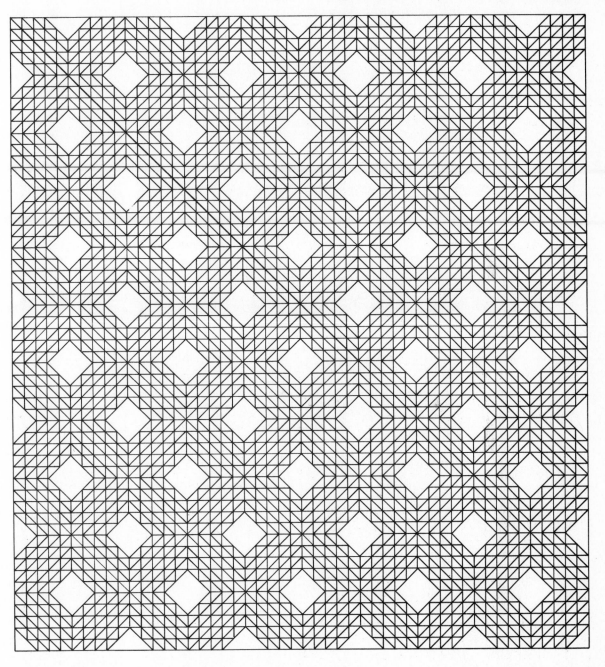

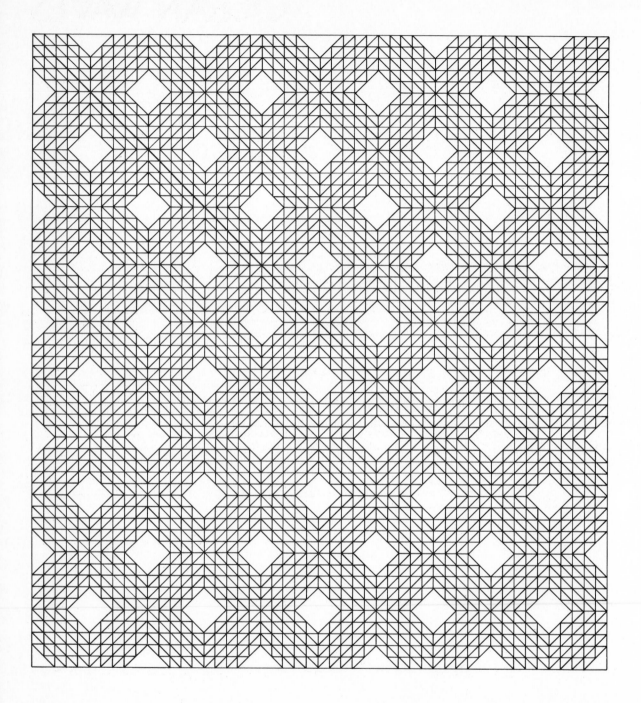

OCEAN WAVES

This quilt is not easy to sew. Each block has three corners to turn.

The finished quilt measures 106¼ × 116¾ inches.

There are fifty-five 15-inch blocks.

Pattern piece	In quilt	In each block
1	4620	84
2	55	1

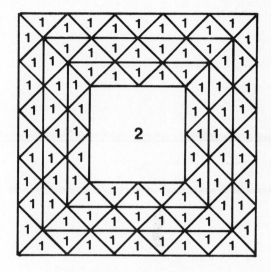

Sew the 1 pieces together in rows of five, seven, and nine, matching notches. There are 220 of each type of row. Each block has four of each type of row. Press seams open.

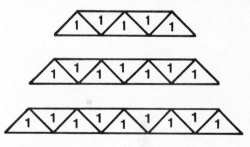

Sew a row of five on top of each row of seven. Sew a row of nine under each row of seven. Press seams open.

Sew a completed 1 section to one side of each 2. Press seams open.

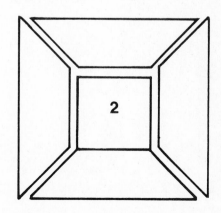

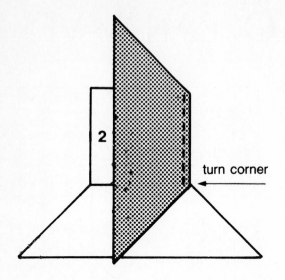

turn corner

Sew another 1 section to each 2, placing it on the right of the 1 section just added. Stop sewing at the seam where 1 meets 2. Clip to the seam and turn the corner. Complete the seam by sewing both 1 sections together. (For instructions in turning corners see page 20.) Press seams open. Working counterclockwise, sew a 1 section to each side of each 2.

When all the blocks are completed, carefully cut ten of them in half diagonally, following the colored-in design. Cut one of the halves into quarters.

Sew the blocks together in diagonal rows as follows:

> one row of one
> one row of two
> one row of three
> one row of four
> one row of five
> one row of six
> one row of seven
> one row of eight
> one row of nine

Press seams open. Lay the rows out on the floor, checking the colored-in design for the proper position of each row.

Pin a half block to the end of each row except at the lower two corners, which require the quarter blocks.

Sew the half and quarter blocks to the ends of the rows. Press seams open. Arrange the rows on the floor again. Sew the rows together, working from one corner. Press seams open.

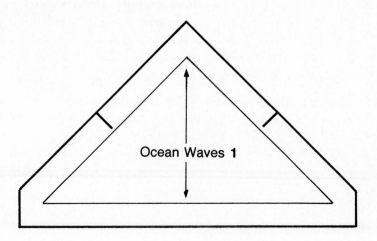

Ocean Waves 1

Ocean Waves **2**

130

PINEAPPLE

132

PINEAPPLE

This quilt is a lot easier to sew than it looks. It is simply built out from the center by adding one piece at a time.

The finished quilt measures 84 × 98 inches.

There are forty-two 14-inch blocks.

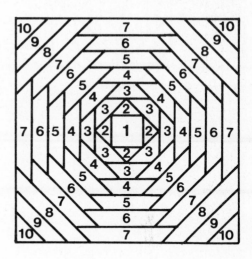

Pattern piece	In quilt	In each block
1	42	1
2	168	4
3	336	8
4	336	8
5	336	8
6	336	8
7	336	8
8	168	4
9	168	4
10	168	4

Sew a 2 to one side of each 1, matching notches. Repeat for the opposite side. Press seams away from the center toward the 2 pieces. Repeat for the other two sides of each 1.

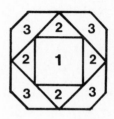

Sew a 3 to one side of each square just completed, matching the notch with the point between the 2 pieces. Repeat for the opposite side. Press seams away from center. Repeat for the other two sides.

Sew a 3 piece to one side between the two 3 pieces, matching the notch with the point between the 3 pieces. Repeat for each side. Press seams away from center.

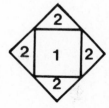

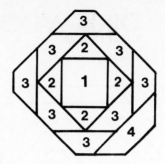

Sew a 4 to one side of each section just completed. Repeat for each of the remaining three sides. Press seams away from center.

Sew a 4 to one corner of each block between two 4 pieces, matching notches. Repeat for each corner. Press seams away from center.

Build the blocks by adding the 5, 6, and 7 pieces in the same way the 3 and 4 pieces were added. Refer often to the diagram of the quilt block. Always press seams away from center.

Sew an 8 to one corner of each block, matching notches. Repeat for the other three corners. Sew a 9 to each 8, matching notches. Sew a 10 to each 9, matching notches. Press seams away from center.

Sew six blocks together to form one horizontal row. Repeat for a total of seven rows. Press seams open.

Sew the rows together to form the quilt top, matching seams at intersections. Press seams open.

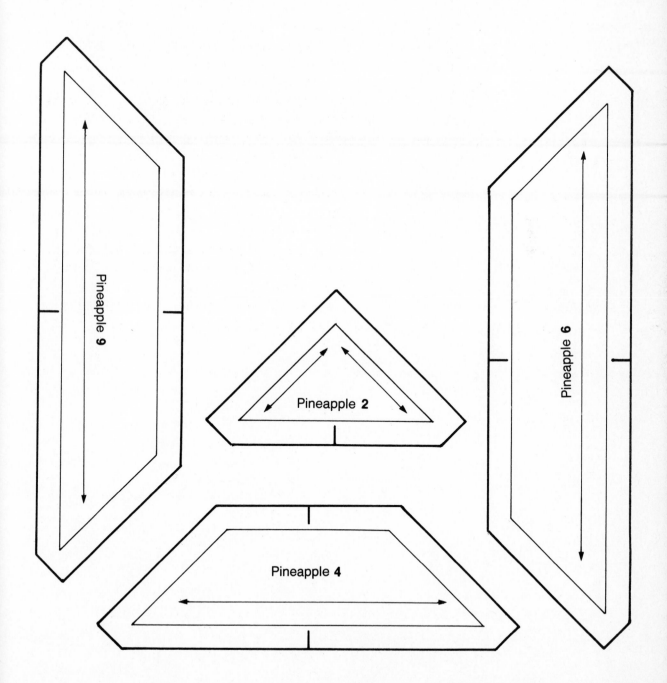

Pineapple 9

Pineapple 6

Pineapple 2

Pineapple 4

135

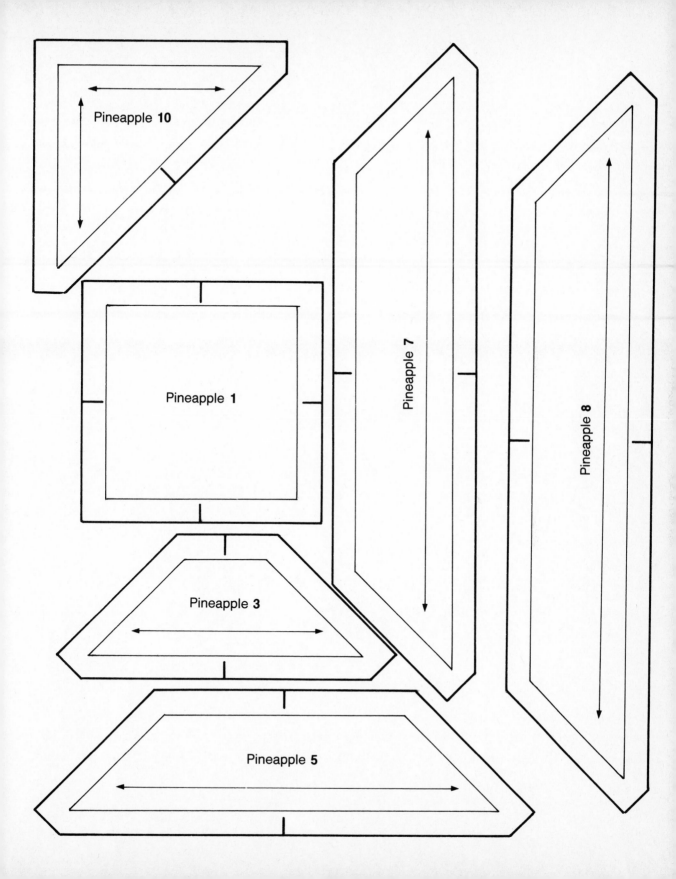

DOUBLE IRISH CHAIN

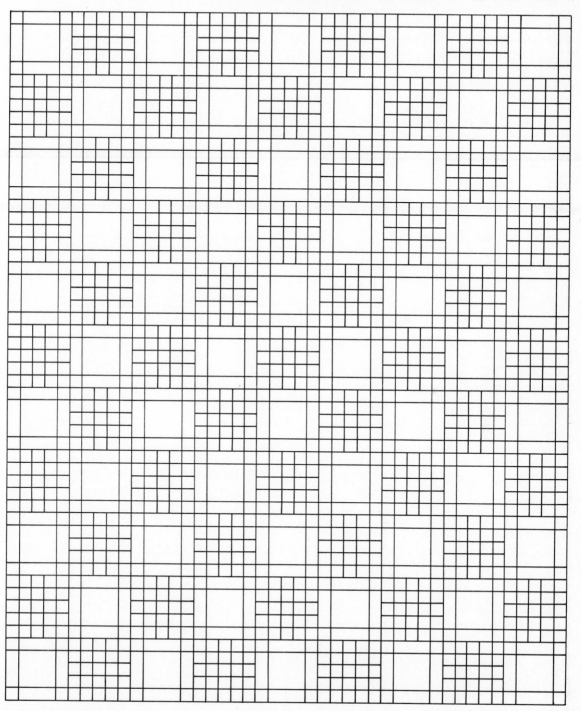

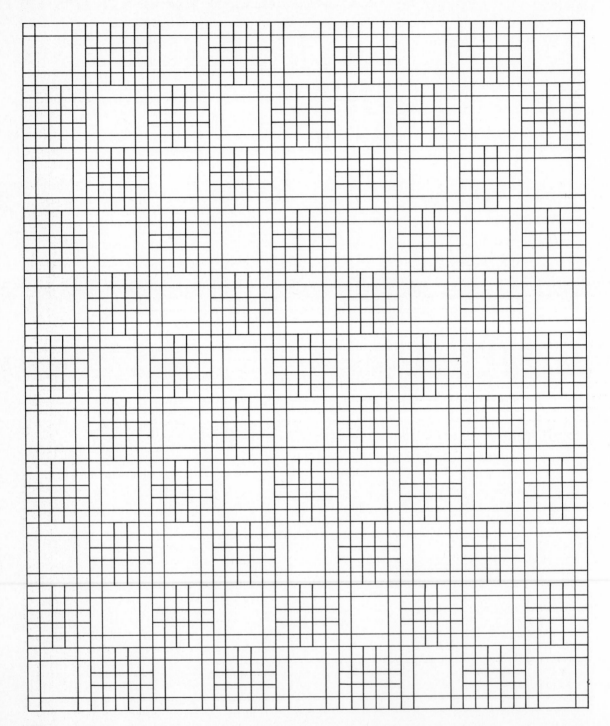

DOUBLE IRISH CHAIN

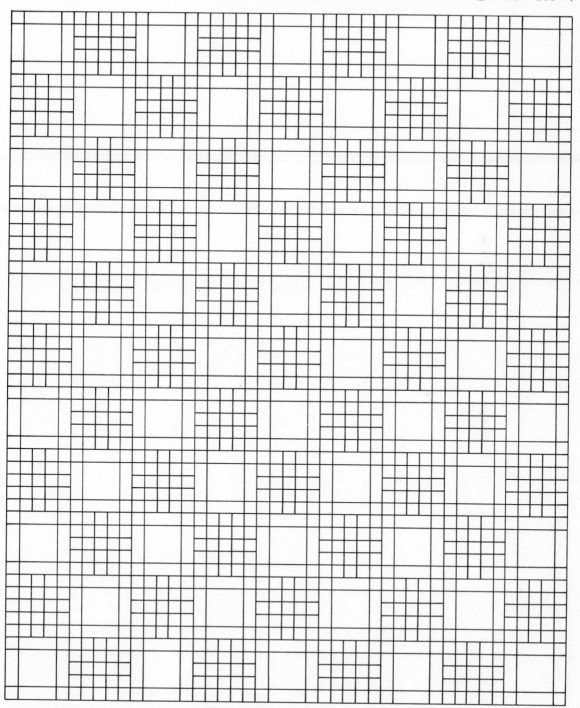

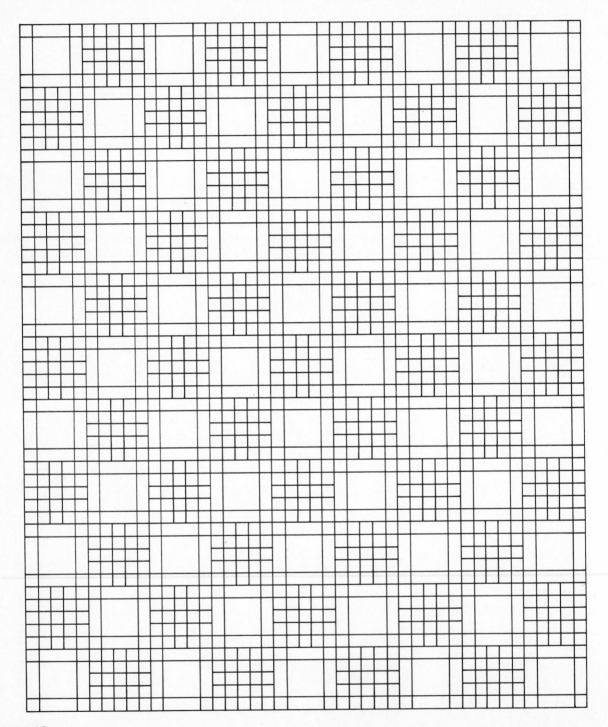

DOUBLE IRISH CHAIN

Although this quilt has many pieces, it is very easy to make.

The finished quilt measures 90 × 110 inches.

There are ninety-nine 10-inch blocks. Fifty are type A and forty-nine are type B.

Pattern piece	In quilt	In type A block	In type B block
1	50	1	
2	200	4	
3	1425	4	25

For blocks A sew a 3 to the end of half (100) of the 2 pieces. Sew another 3 to the other end of these 2 pieces. Press seams open.

Sew a 2 to one side of each 1. Sew a 2 to the opposite side of each 1. Press seams open.

Sew a 3-2-3 section to one side of each 2-1-2 section. Sew another 3-2-3 section to the other side. Press seams open.

For blocks B select the 3 pieces according to color scheme. Sew five together to form one row. Repeat for five rows. Press seams open. Sew the rows together.

Following the colored-in design, sew five blocks of type A to four blocks of type B, alternating them so a type A block is on either end of the row. Repeat, making six rows in all.

Sew four blocks of type A to five blocks of type B, alternating them so that a type B block is on either end of the row. Repeat, making five rows in all. Press seams open for all rows.

Sew these rows together so that the type A and B blocks alternate throughout. Match seams at intersections. Press seams open.

3	2	3
2	1	2
3	2	3

A

3	3	3	3	3
3	3	3	3	3
3	3	3	3	3
3	3	3	3	3
3	3	3	3	3

B

Double Irish Chain **1**

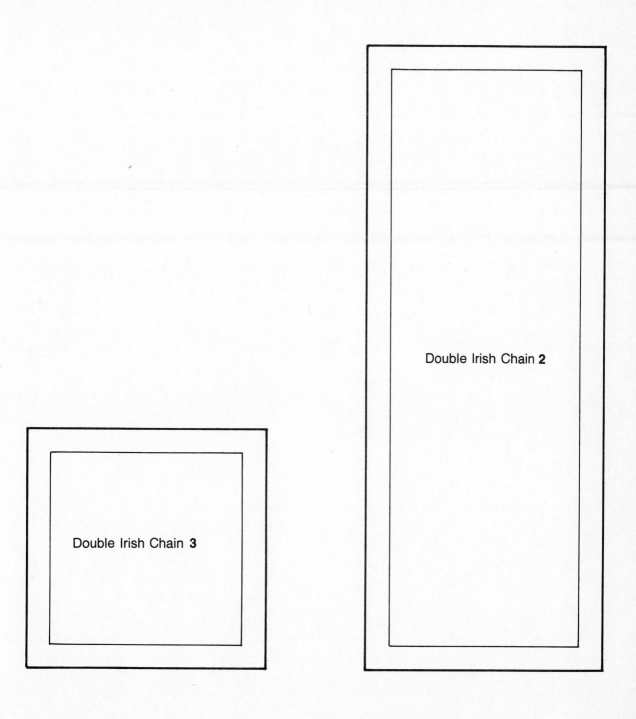

Double Irish Chain **2**

Double Irish Chain **3**

SQUARE AND COMPASS

SQUARE AND COMPASS

152

SQUARE AND COMPASS

This quilt is for the experienced sewer. It has many set-in curves.

The finished quilt measures 72 × 84 inches.

There are forty-two 12-inch blocks.

Pattern piece	In quilt	In each block
1	336	8
2	336	8
3	672	16

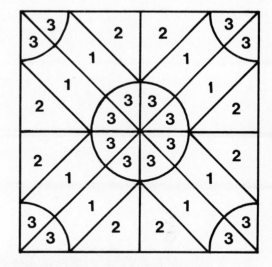

Sew two 1 pieces together along their short straight sides, matching notches. Press seams open.

Sew a 2 to a straight side of each 1-1 section, matching notches. Repeat for the other straight side. Press seams open.

Sew two 3 pieces together along one of their straight sides. Press seams open.

Set a 3-3 section into the curve at one end of each 1-2 section, matching notches. (For instructions in sewing curves see page 22.) Repeat for the other end of each 1-2 section. *Note:* It is easier to assemble the circles of the quilt design a quarter at a time than to try to set in a full circle. Press seams toward 1-2 sections.

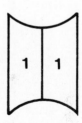

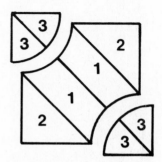

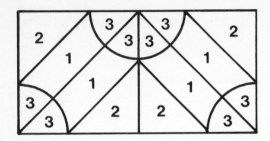

Sew two 1-2-3 sections together to form a half block. The four 3 pieces in this half block meet at one end, forming a semicircle. When sewing, be sure to match seams at the intersections. Press seams open.

Sew the halves together into blocks, matching seams at the intersections and the center. Press seams open.

Sew six blocks together to form one horizontal row. Repeat for a total of seven rows. Press seams open.

Sew the rows together to form the quilt top, matching seams at the intersections. Press seams open.

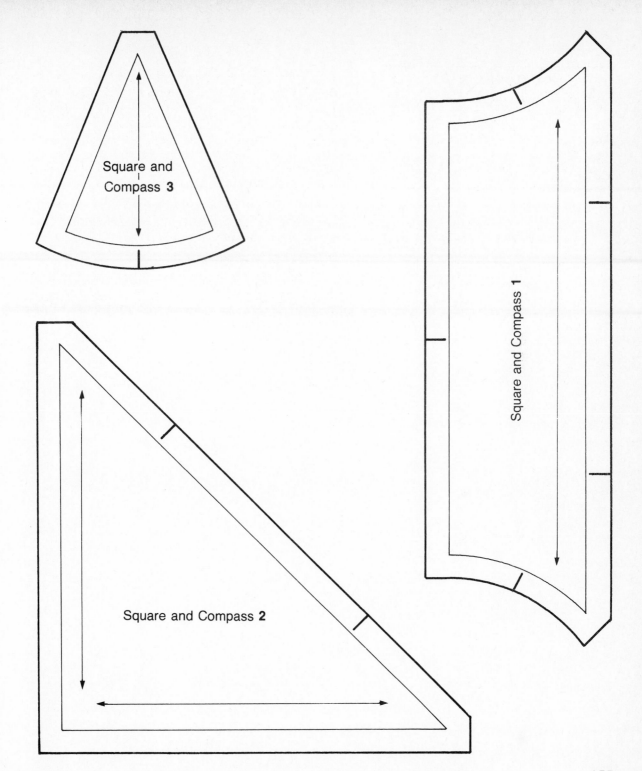

Square and Compass **3**

Square and Compass 1

Square and Compass **2**

LOG CABIN

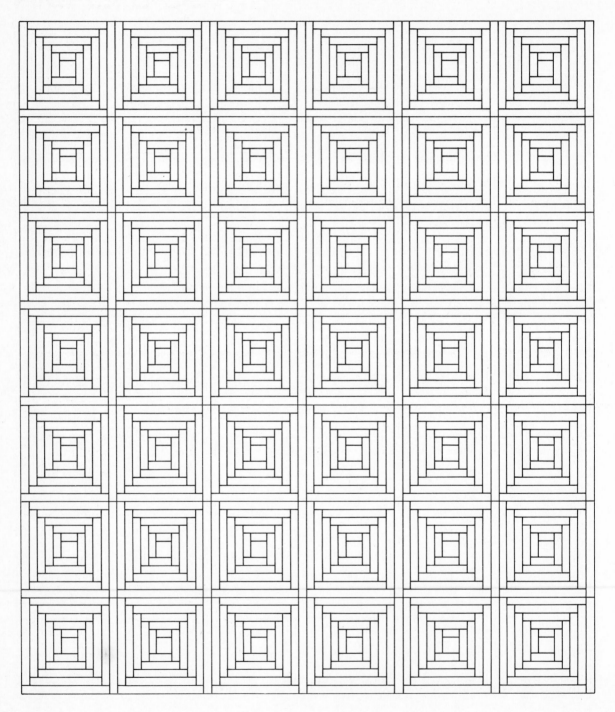

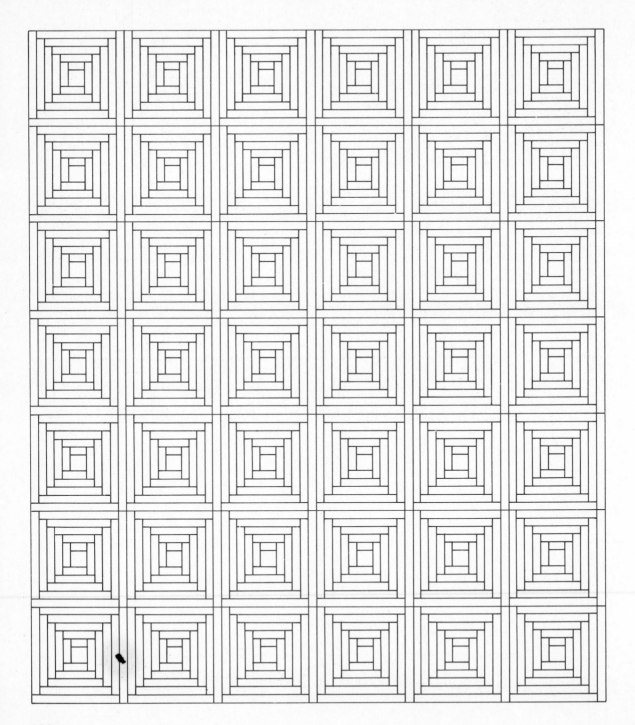

LOG CABIN

This is an easy quilt to make, and the number of possibilities for color variation is enormous.

The finished quilt measures 54 × 63 inches.

There are forty-two 9-inch blocks.

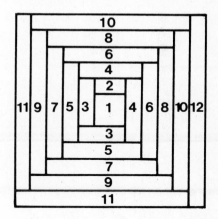

Pattern piece	In quilt	In each block
1	42	1
2	42	1
3	84	2
4	84	2
5	84	2
6	84	2
7	84	2
8	84	2
9	84	2
10	84	2
11	84	2
12	42	1

Sew a 2 to each 1. Press seams open.

Sew a 3 to the left side of each 1-2 section. Press seams open.

Continue working counterclockwise from the center out, following the diagram for the quilt block. Always add the next piece at right angles to the piece just sewed on. Press all seams open.

When the blocks are completed, sew six together to form one row of horizontal blocks. Repeat for a total of seven rows. Press seams open.

Sew the seven rows together to form quilt top. Press seams open.

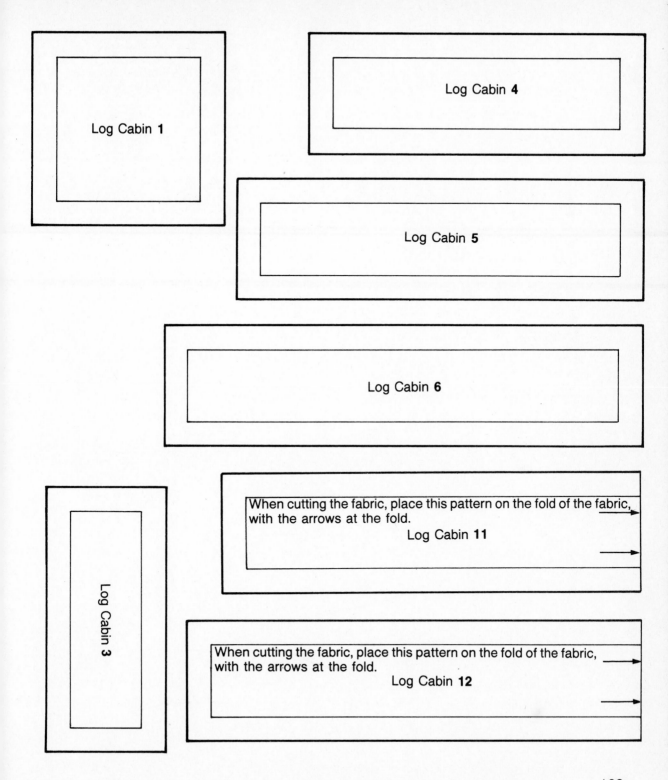

Log Cabin **1**

Log Cabin **4**

Log Cabin **5**

Log Cabin **6**

Log Cabin **3**

When cutting the fabric, place this pattern on the fold of the fabric, with the arrows at the fold.

Log Cabin **11**

When cutting the fabric, place this pattern on the fold of the fabric, with the arrows at the fold.

Log Cabin **12**

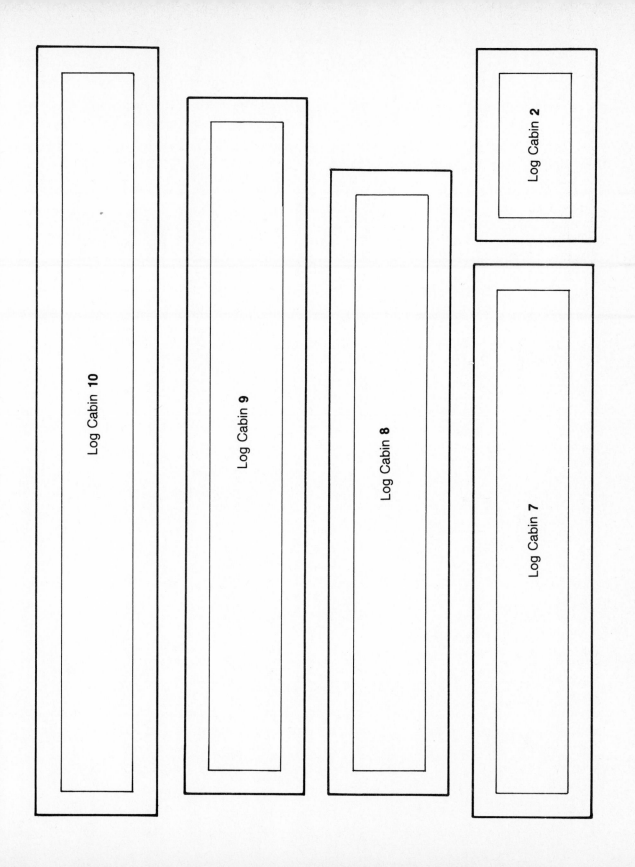

Log Cabin **10**

Log Cabin **9**

Log Cabin **8**

Log Cabin **7**

Log Cabin **2**

ROAD TO CALIFORNIA

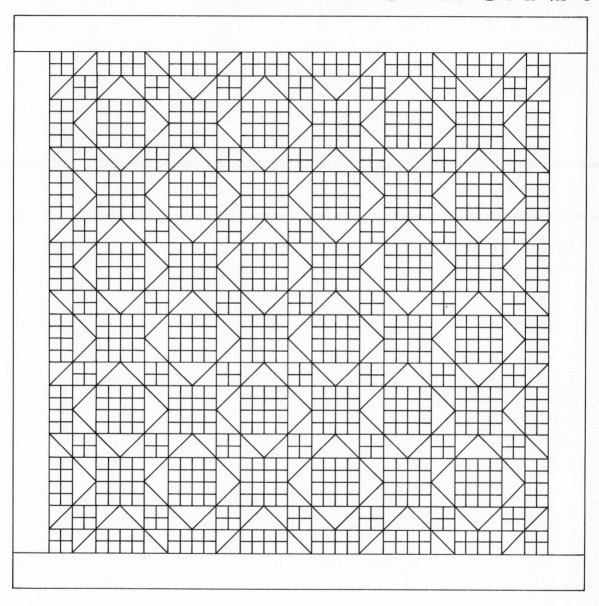

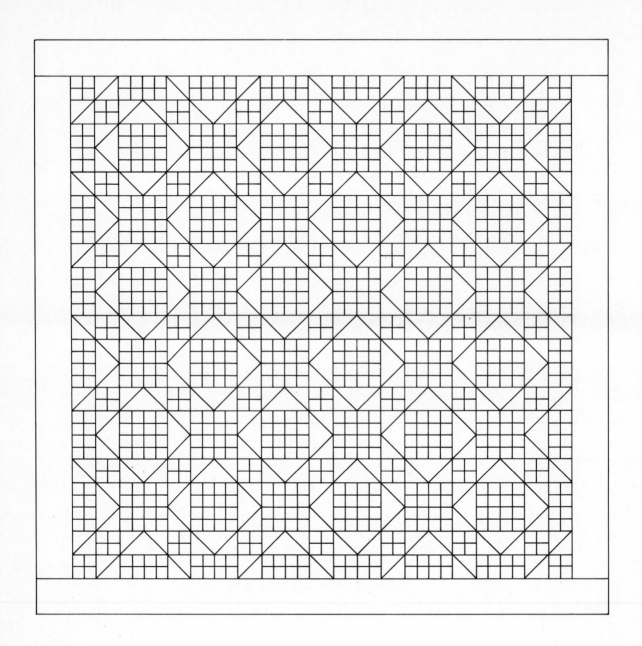

ROAD TO CALIFORNIA

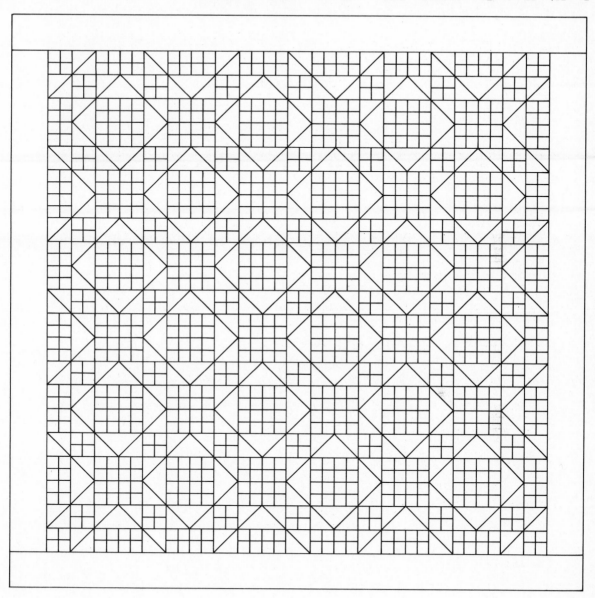

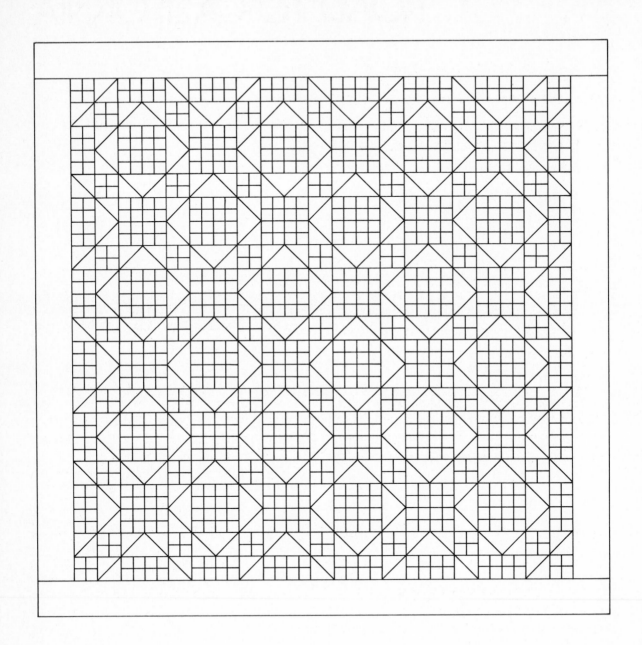

ROAD TO CALIFORNIA

This is a very easy quilt to make.

The finished quilt measures 96 × 96 inches.

This design is not made from multiples of one block but from an arrangement of five different kinds of sections.

Pattern piece	In quilt
1	980
2	224
3	84

Cut two border pieces 6½ × 84½ inches and two pieces 6½ × 96½ inches.

Sew all the 1 pieces together in groups of two. Press seams open. Sew these groups together, matching seams at intersections, into 245 squares of four 1 pieces. Set fifty-three of these sections aside.

Sew the remaining 192 sections together into ninety-six rectangles of eight 1 pieces. Press seams open. Set twenty-four of these sections aside.

Sew seventy-two of these rectangular sections together, matching seams at intersections, into thirty-six squares of sixteen 1 pieces. Press seams open.

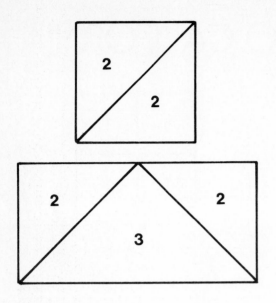

Sew fifty-six 2 pieces together into twenty-eight squares of two 2 pieces, matching notches. Press seams open.

Sew a 2 to one side of each 3, matching notches. Press seams open. Repeat for the other side.

Arrange all sections on the floor according to color scheme. Check diagram of full quilt to be sure that all sections are in their proper places and that triangles are pointing in the proper direction.

Sew the sections together in horizontal rows. Press seams open.

Sew the rows together, matching seams at intersections, to form the quilt top. Press seams open.

Sew the two 6½- × 84½-inch borders to opposite sides of the quilt top. Press seams toward borders. Sew the two 6½- × 96½-inch borders to the top and bottom. Press seams toward borders.

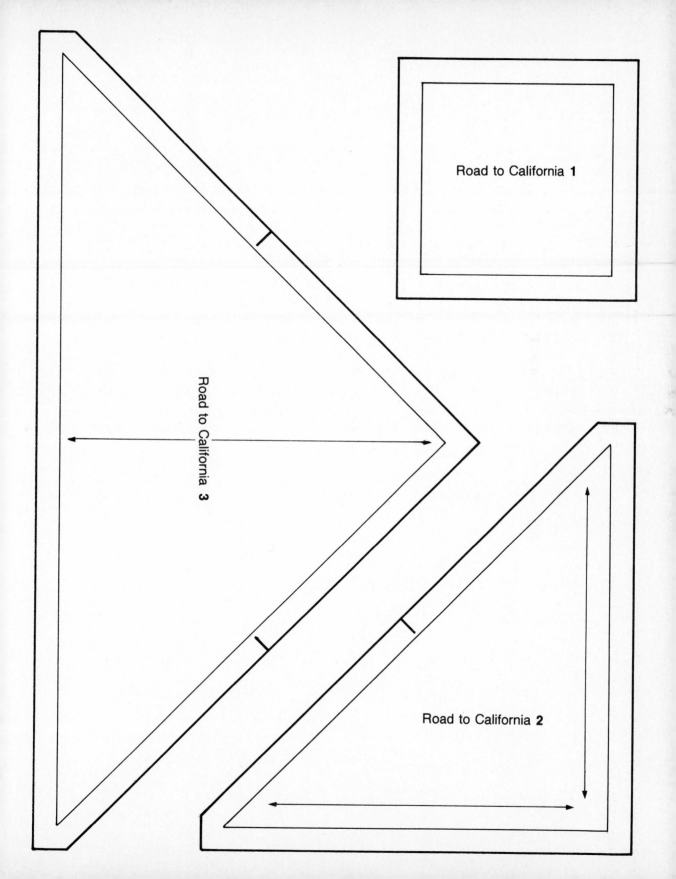

Road to California 1

Road to California 3

Road to California 2

MEXICAN STAR

This quilt is not difficult to sew, but assembling the blocks is tricky. Study the diagrams for the two types of quilt blocks carefully before sewing.

The finished quilt measures 60 × 72 inches.

There are sixty 8½-inch blocks. Thirty-five of the blocks are type A and twenty-five are type B.

Pattern piece	In quilt	In each block
1	60	1
2	240	4
3	180	3
4	120	2
5	120	2

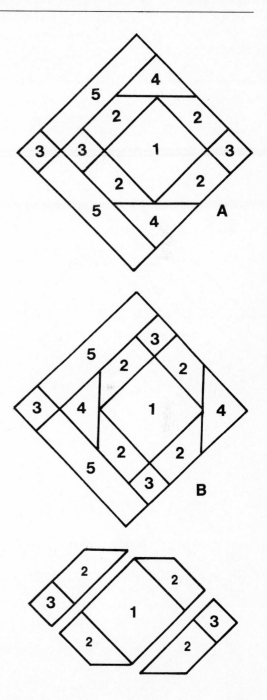

Cut the 2 pieces from fabric folded right sides together so that, when cut, half of them are mirror images of the other half. Keep the two kinds separate.

Sew a 2 to one side of each 1 by lining up the square end of 2 to 1. Press seams open. Repeat for the opposite side of each 1, using the 2 piece that is a mirror image of the attached 2.

Sew a 3 to the square end of each remaining 2. Press seams open.

Sew the longer side of a 2-3 section to one side of each 2-1-2 section, matching seams at the intersection. In the same way, sew a 2-3 (mirror image) section to the opposite side of each 2-1-2 section. Press seams open.

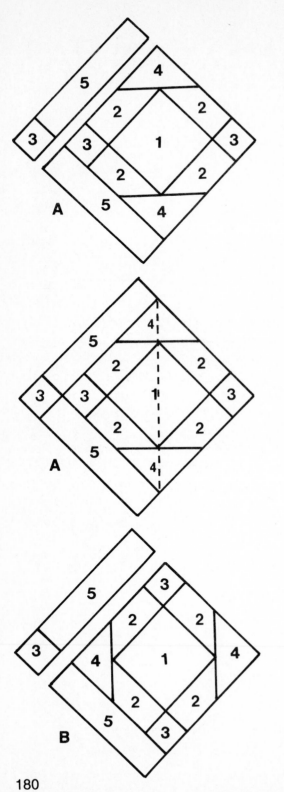

Sew a 4 to fill out the corner of each 1-2-3 section, matching notches. Repeat for the opposite corner. Press seams open.

To construct the type A block, sew a 5 to the 3-2-4 side of thirty-five blocks. Check the diagram for the type A block before sewing, using the position of the 4 piece to help you add the 5 piece to the correct side. Press seams open.

Sew a 3 to the end of sixty 5 pieces. Press seams open. Sew thirty-five 3-5 sections to the side adjacent to the 5 piece in the thirty-five type A blocks so that the 3 pieces are at the corner between the 5 pieces. Press seams open.

Carefully mark and cut eleven type A blocks so that the cut divides the 1 pieces diagonally in half.

To construct the type B block, sew a 5 to the 4-2-3 side of the remaining twenty-five blocks, checking the diagram of the type B block before sewing. Press seams open.

Sew the remaining 3-5 sections to the type B blocks so that the 3 pieces are at the corner between the 5 pieces.

Keeping the 3-5 sections of the blocks on the left side, and alternating the A and B blocks, sew the blocks together in diagonal rows as follows:

> two rows of two
> two rows of four
> two rows of six
> two rows of eight
> one row of nine, starting and
> ending this row with a B block

Check diagram for the full quilt to be sure blocks are in their proper place. Press seams open.

Lay the rows diagonally on the floor in their proper order, following the design you have colored in. Pin the half-blocks to the ends of the rows, checking the design carefully to see that the half-blocks face in the proper direction. Sew them in place. Press seams open and return the rows to their proper order on the floor.

Working from one corner, sew each row to the next, matching seams at intersections. Press seams open.

Mexican Star **1**

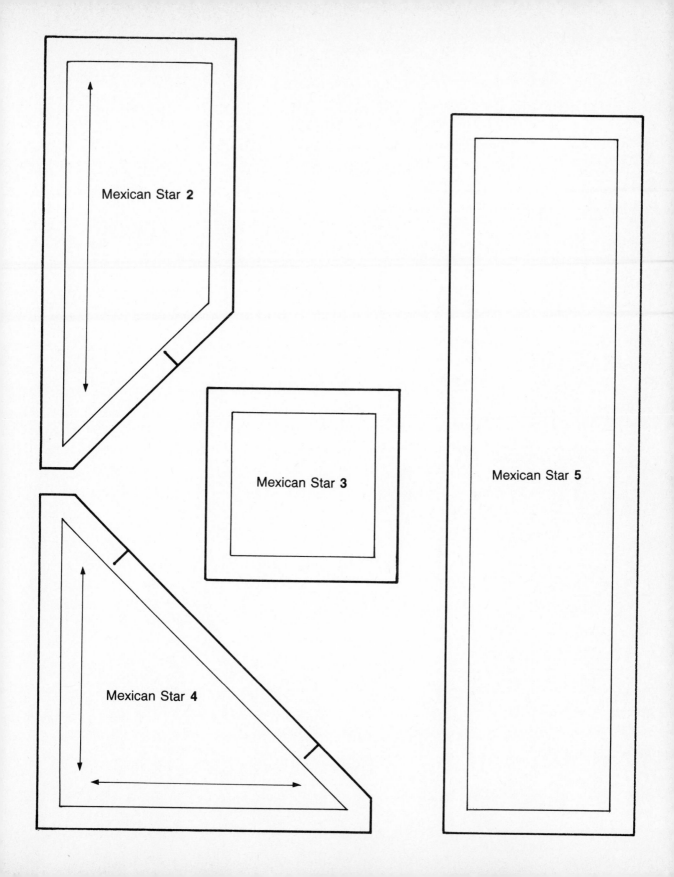

SHOO FLY

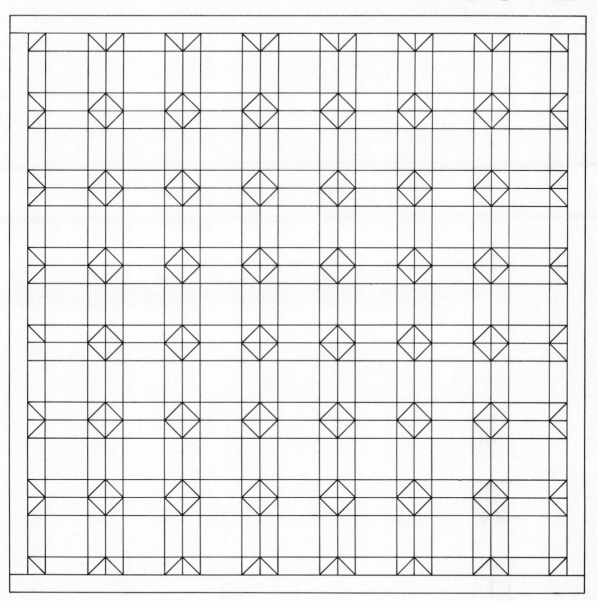

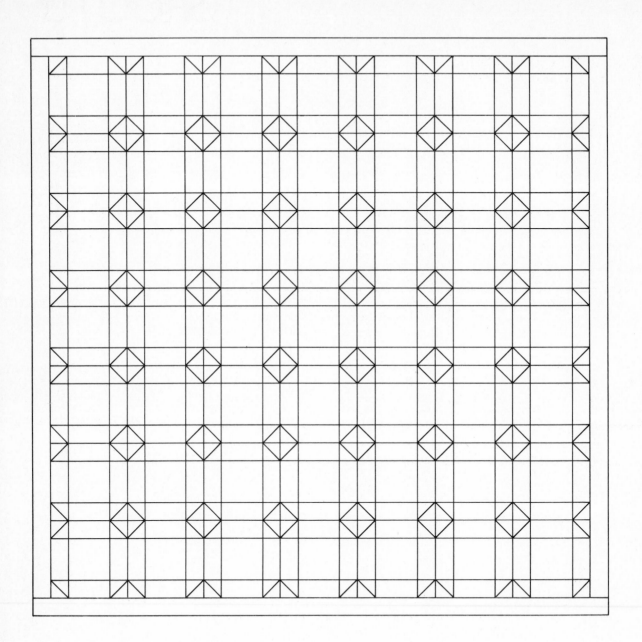

SHOO FLY

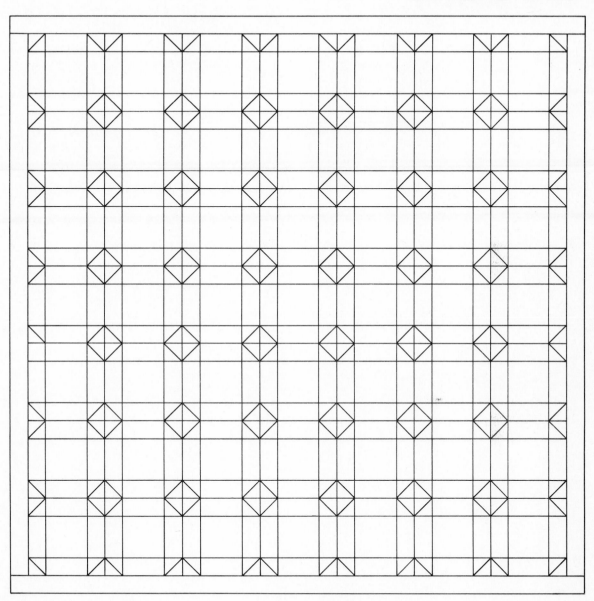

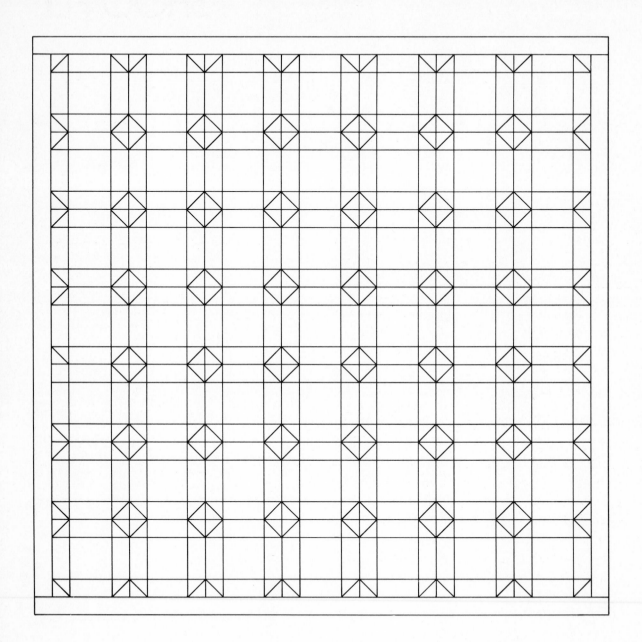

SHOO FLY

This is a very easy quilt to make.

The finished quilt measures 78½ × 78½ inches, including borders.

There are forty-nine 10½-inch blocks.

Pattern piece	In quilt	In each block
1	392	8
2	196	4
3	49	1

Cut two 3- × 74-inch border pieces and two 3- × 79-inch pieces.

Sew all the 1 pieces together, matching notches. Press seams open.

Sew a 2 to one side of each 3. Repeat for the opposite side. Press seams open.

Sew one of the 1-1 sections to one end of each of the remaining 2 pieces, checking diagram to be sure the bias seam falls in the proper direction. Repeat for the other end of each 2. Press seams open.

Sew a 1-2-1 section across the top of each 2-3-2 section, matching seams at intersections.

Sew a 1-2-1 section to the bottom, also matching seams. Press seams open.

Sew seven blocks together to form one row. Repeat for a total of seven rows. Press seams open.

Sew the seven rows together, matching seams at intersections. Press seams open.

Sew the two 3- × 74-inch borders to each side of the quilt top. Press seams toward borders. Sew the two 3- × 79-inch borders to the top and bottom. Press seams toward borders.

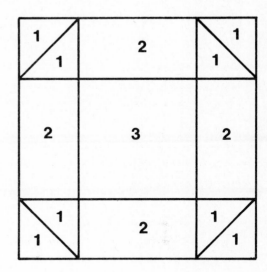

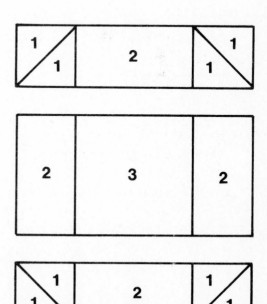

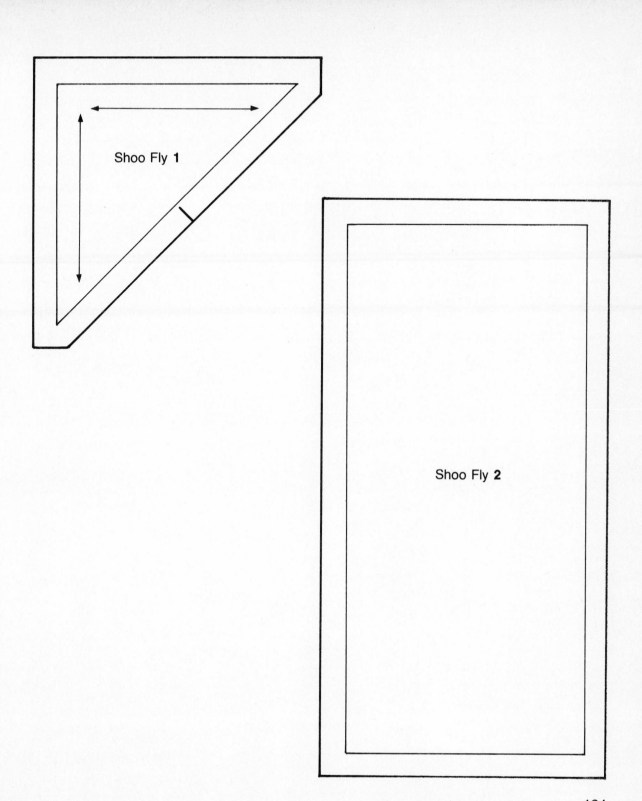

Shoo Fly **1**

Shoo Fly **2**

191

Shoo Fly **3**

HEXAGON

196

HEXAGON

HEXAGON

This quilt is difficult and slow to sew because it is made entirely by turning corners. But you might want to try this one because of its many design possibilities. You can treat it as a mosaic, you can emphasize the diagonals formed by the hexagons, or you can color in some of the hexagons to form letters making a name, a monogram, a motto, or even "Happy Birthday."

The finished quilt measures 100 × 112 inches.

There are 1,056 3⅓- × 4-inch hexagons. The edges of the quilt can be uneven, following the outline of the hexagons, or they can be made straight by trimming.

There are two ways to assemble the quilt.

Method 1: In this method the hexagons are sewn together to make circles. The numbers in the diagram show the order of assembly. They do not refer to pattern piece number.

Sew two hexagons together. Press seams open. Sew the third hexagon to the first two. Start by sewing the first to the third. Stop at the seam that joins the first two. Clip to the seam and turn the corner to finish the seam. (For directions in turning corners, see page 20.) Press seams open.

Working counterclockwise, add hexagons until six surround the one in the center. Build the entire quilt from the center out, or repeat the instructions to form many small circles that are joined together in the same way as the seven single hexagons were joined to form a circle. Study your color scheme to see which might be easier for you.

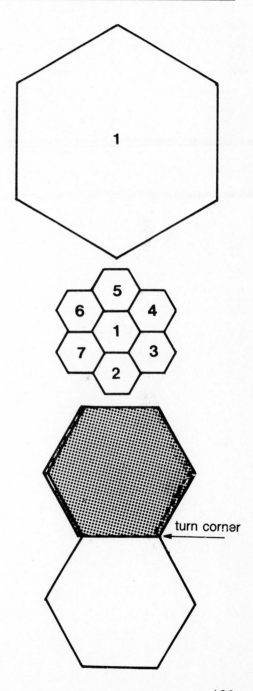

turn corner

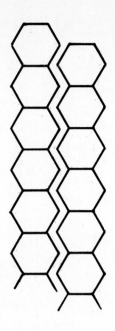

Method 2: In this method the hexagons are assembled in rows and the rows are sewed together.

Sew thirty-two hexagons together to form one vertical row. Repeat for thirty-three rows. Press seams open. Sew these rows together. A corner will be turned when each hexagon is joined to one in the next row. Press seams open.

Either trim off the uneven outside edges to form straight sides or leave the edges as they are. For final quilt assembly see pages 26–28. If you have left the quilt edges untrimmed, you will have to sew turned corners at each hexagon if you assemble the final quilt according to the first method. If you finish the quilt with bias seam binding, follow the outlines of the hexagon with the binding.

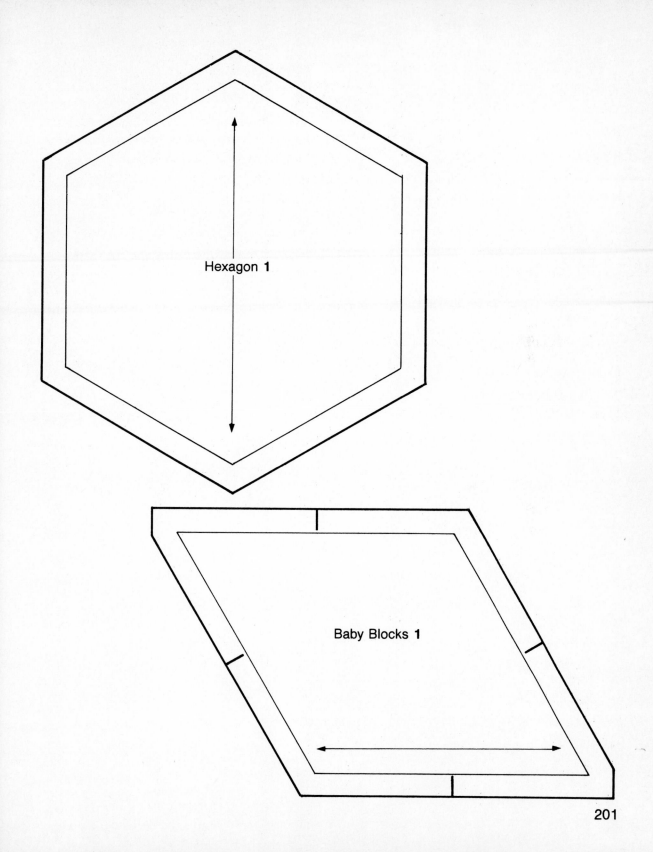

Hexagon **1**

Baby Blocks **1**

BABY BLOCKS

BABY BLOCKS

206

BABY BLOCKS

This is not a good quilt for the beginning sewer. It is made entirely by sewing turned corners.

The finished quilt measures 60 × 83½ inches.

There are 228 5- × 5¾-inch blocks. The quilt has straight sides and a jagged top and bottom edge.

Pattern piece	In quilt	In each block
1	684	3

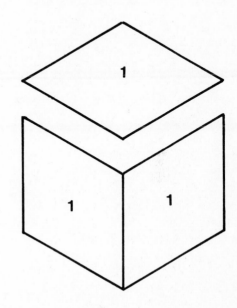

The pattern piece for Baby Blocks is printed on page 201.

Sew two 1 pieces together, matching notches.

Sew a 1 to the inside edge of the 1-1 section, matching notches. Stop at the seam joining the first two 1 pieces. Clip to seam and finish off seam by sewing the other side of 1 to the left 1 piece. (For instructions in turning corners see page 20.) Repeat until all 228 blocks are assembled. Press seams open. Cut nine blocks in half.

The finished blocks are hexagons. They are joined together to form the quilt top in exactly the same way as is the Hexagon quilt. They can be sewn together in circles or in rows.

For directions in sewing together in circles, see Method 1 in the Hexagon instructions, page 199. Following your colored-in design, sew the half blocks in the proper places on the sides of the quilt.

To sew the blocks together in rows, sew twelve blocks together to form one horizontal

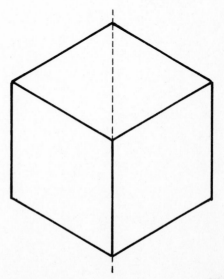

row. Repeat for a total of ten rows. Sew eleven blocks together to form one horizontal row. Repeat for a total of nine rows. Sew the half blocks to the ends of each of the nine rows of eleven blocks. Press seams open. Sew the rows together, alternating the two types of rows, following the diagram of the full quilt.

For final assembly see pages 26–28. If you assemble the quilt according to the first method, you will have to sew turned corners at the top and bottom edges of the quilt. If you finish the quilt with bias seam binding, follow the outlines of the hexagon on the top and bottom edges with the binding.

TULIP

This quilt is not simple to make because some of the corners have to be turned.

The finished quilt measures 72 × 91 inches.

There are forty-two tulip blocks and forty-two plain. They are separated by sixty-six squares. There are thirty-four triangles at the sides and four triangles at the corners.

Pattern piece	In quilt	In each block
1	168	4
2	168	4
3	42	1
4	84	2
5	42	1
6	84	2
7	84	2
8	84	2
9	84	2
10	42	
11	66	
12	34	
13	4	

Cut the 4, 6, 7, and 8 pattern pieces from fabric folded right sides together so that the pieces, when cut, are mirror images of each other.

Sew two 1 pieces together. Repeat until all 1 pieces are sewn together in groups of two. Press seams open. Sew them together in groups of four to form squares.

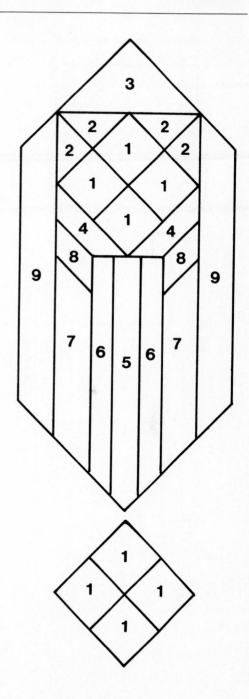

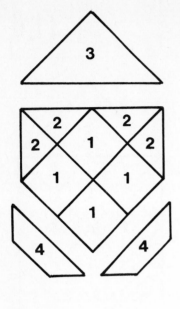

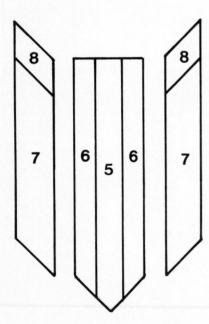

Sew the 2 pieces together in groups of two along their shorter sides. Press seams open.

Sew a 2-2 section to one side of each 1 group, matching intersecting seams. Press seams open. Sew a 2-2 section to the side immediately next to the side of each 1 group just completed. Press seams open.

Sew a 4 to one of the remaining sides of the 1 section. Press seams open. Sew a 4 to the last side of the 1 section. Press seams open.

Sew a 3 on top of each of the 1-2 sections just completed. Press seams open.

Sew a 6 to one side of each 5, matching notches. Repeat for the other side of each 5. Press seams open.

Sew an 8 to the top of each 7, matching notches. Press seams open.

Sew a 7-8 section to one side of each 6-5-6 section, matching notches. Repeat for the other side. Press seams open.

Pin a 1-2-3-4 section into a 5-6-7-8 section, matching notches and corners. Join by sewing 4 to 8 and stop at the corner where 4, 8, and 6 meet. Turn the corner, sew across the 5 and 6 pieces, and stop at the next corner where 4, 8, and 6 meet. Turn the corner and complete the tulip section by sewing 4 and 8 together. (For instructions in turning corners see page 20.) Press seams toward the 5-6-7-8 portion.

Sew a 9 to one side of each of the tulip sections just completed. Sew a 9 to the other side. Press seams toward 9.

To assemble the blocks, sew an 11 to the upper right side of thirty-three tulip blocks and an 11 to the upper right side of thirty-three plain blocks (pattern piece 10). Press seams open.

Arrange the tulip blocks that are sewn to the 11 pieces into diagonal rows as follows:

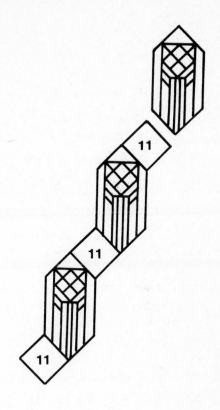

> one row of one
> one row of two
> one row of three
> one row of four
> one row of five
> three rows of six

Sew the bottom left sides of the tulip blocks to the top right sides of the 11 pieces. Sew a tulip section to the top of each diagonal row.

Assemble diagonal rows of plain blocks in the same way.

Lay the rows out on the floor according to the diagram of the full quilt, alternating the tulip and plain rows. Place the one remaining tulip block and one remaining plain block in their proper places at the opposite corners of the quilt. Following the diagram carefully, pin the 12 (end) pieces to the ends of each row, except for the four corners, which require the 13 pieces.

Sew the corner and end pieces in place. Press seams open. Return the rows to their former places on the floor. They are now ready to be sewn to each other.

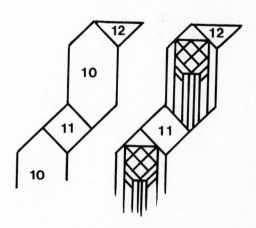

Work from one corner of the quilt top to the other, adding one row at a time. (For instructions in turning corners see page 20.) Press each seam open.

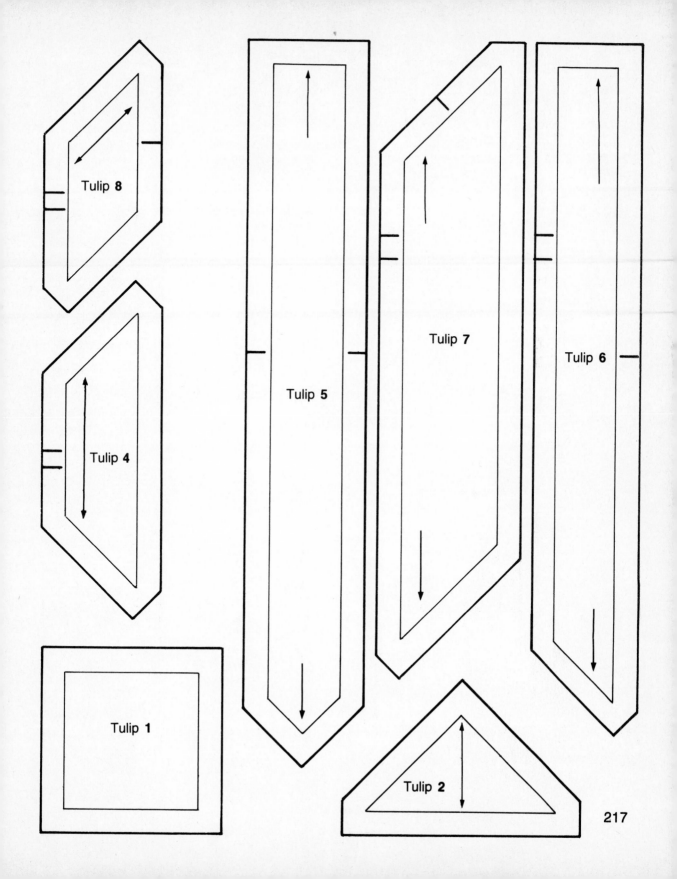

Tulip 8

Tulip 5

Tulip 7

Tulip 6

Tulip 4

Tulip 1

Tulip 2

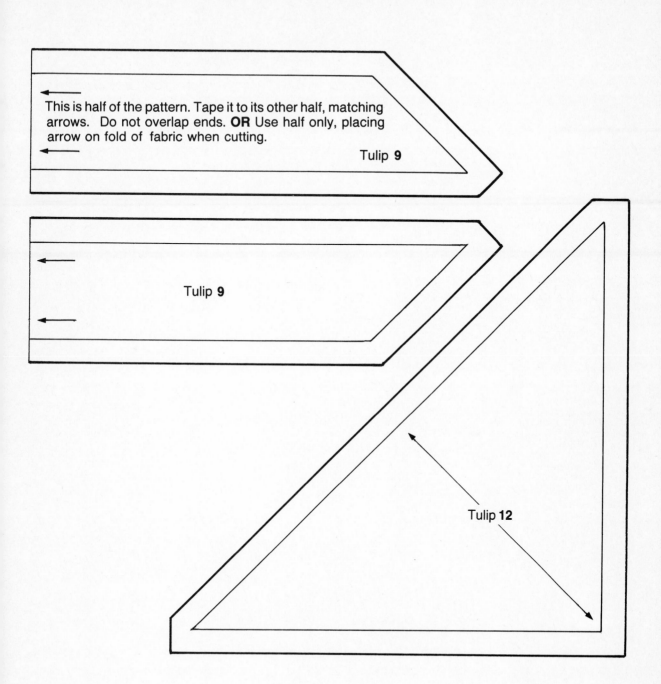

This is half of the pattern. Tape it to its other half, matching arrows. Do not overlap ends. **OR** Use half only, placing arrow on fold of fabric when cutting.

Tulip **9**

Tulip **9**

Tulip **12**

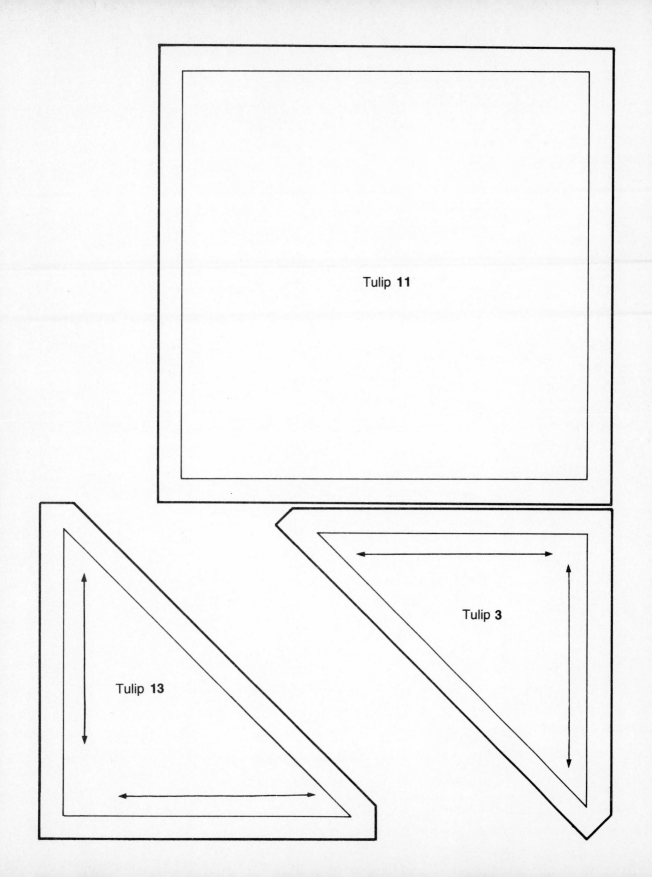

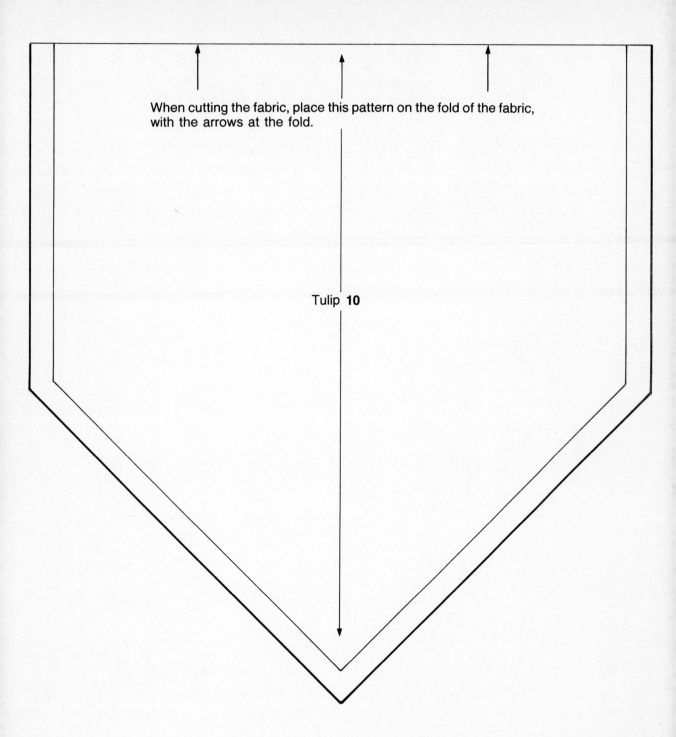

When cutting the fabric, place this pattern on the fold of the fabric, with the arrows at the fold.

Tulip **10**

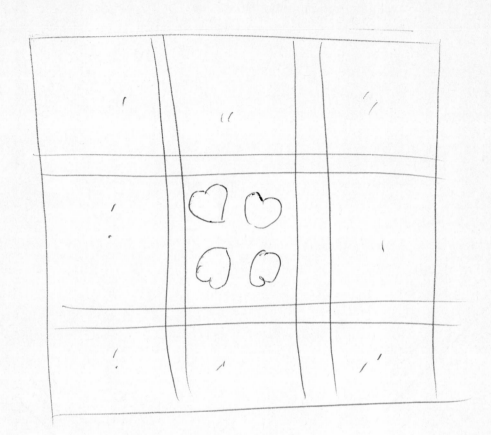